031000

D0489362

SPREADING THE NEWS

SPREADING THE NEWS

A guide to media reform

by Frank Allaun

with a Foreword by James Curran

SPOKESMAN
for the Campaign for Press and
Broadcasting Freedom

037988

First published in 1988 by:
Spokesman
Bertrand Russell House
Gamble Street
Nottingham, England
for the Campaign for Press and Broadcasting Freedom

British Library Cataloguing in Publication Data

Allaun, Frank
  Spreading the news: a guide to media reform.
  1. Mass media
  I. Title
  302.2'34

  ISBN 0-85124-488-2
  ISBN 0-85124-498-X

Printed by the Russell Press Ltd, Nottingham
(Tel. 0602 784505)

Contents

Acknowledgements

This book would not have been completed without the encouragement and assistance of Mike Power of the Campaign for Press and Broadcasting Freedom, and James Curran of Goldsmiths College, London, who has kindly agreed to write the Foreword. My thanks also to Ken Fleet and everybody at Spokesman for their efficiency and goodwill.

Foreword

The general shape of this book is as follows. The first section (chapters 1 and 2) provides a general survey of the British press, TV and radio. The second section (chapters 3, 4 and 5) examines in greater detail particular aspects of the media — the dirty tricks of journalism, and attempts to combat them; the impact of new technology; legal and other constraints. The last section (chapters 7, 8 and 9) is devoted to a discussion of media policy.

The publication of this book is well timed. It comes at a crucial watershed in the development of the British media.

Within the next eighteen months, the British public will have more TV channels than national dailies to choose from. The technology also now exists for encrypting programmes and channels so that people can pay directly for what they view in much the way that they subscribe to a newspaper or magazine. The way is thus open to remodel TV on the competitive and unregulated, private enterprise lines of the press.

There is unused capacity within the radio system. Vacancies exist on the airwave frequencies for a large increase in the number of local radio stations. By ending 'simulcasting' — the broadcast of the same service on different frequencies — room can be created for additional national radio channels. Furthermore, commercial radio is relatively underdeveloped in Britain compared with a number of other capitalist countries, and there is clearly scope for generating more radio advertising to finance an expansion of the system.

There are thus wide open opportunities for a radical, Conservative government to fundamentally restructure British broadcasting. The pressures and temptations for them to do so are enormous. The modern Conservative Party has close connections with the leading corporations in the communications industry, many of which have been pressing for the deregulation of commercial broadcasting and the privatisation of the BBC. The government is committed to the 'free market' as its central philosophy, and is thus predisposed to allow the market a dominant role in the organisation of broadcasting. It also has a political motive for deregulating broadcasting since this would result in the extension of big business control over TV and radio and the removal of the public service requirements of balance and accuracy. In a deregulated form, broadcasting would exhibit many of the openly right-wing prejudices of the press.

But there are also countervailing influences within the Conservative party tugging in the opposite direction. There is growing concern, expressed with particular vehemence in the heartlands of Conservative England, that unrestricted competition will result in increased displays of indecency and violence on television. This concern has already resulted in the introduction of extensive censorship of videos. It will find new expression shortly in the establishment of a Broadcasting Standards Council, whose role will be to pressurise the broadcasting authorities into imposing tougher guidelines on sex and violence. And the government is now taking an active role in seeking a pan-European agreement, through the Council of Europe Convention, to impose 'programme standards' on satellite broadcasters principally in order to prevent the commercial exploitation of sex and violence. The thrust of Conservative moral entrepreneurship is thus to increase rather than to reduce certain forms of programme regulation.

There also persists within the Conservative party a Reithian tradition committed to maintaining British cultural traditions, and sustaining a diversity of broadcasting output including minority programmes which would be pushed into off-peak hours or would not be made in a totally commercial system. As some Conservative commentators have rightly acknowledged, the market in broadcasting is distorted by the fact that broadcasting organisations can put on extra 'sales' in terms of increased ratings at a negligible additional cost. This powerfully reinforces commercial pressures to aim for the middle market with common denominator programmes. This is one reason why the Conservative Home Secretary, Douglas Hurd, has required the new commercial national radio channels to provide 'a diverse programme service calculated to appeal to a variety of tastes and interests and not limited to a single format'. Whether this remit is still adhered to under the new radio authority which is to have a 'light touch', remains to be seen.

The government is also inhibited by financial considerations from giving the green light to the rapid expansion of broadcasting on a deregulated basis. There is only a finite amount of additional advertising that an increase in the number of media outlets will generate. Too rapid an acceleration in the number of advertising funded TV channels could lead to the fragmentation of its audience and economic base.This could result in TV organisations spending much less money on their programmes, and so could reduce their quality. It was principally the fear that there was not enough advertising to go round which ultimately persuaded the government, following the Peacock Committee report (1986), not to introduce advertising in the BBC.

The balance of forces and arguments in play over the development of broadcasting is thus not overwhelmingly tilted to one side even with a radical, Conservative government in charge. The expansion of broadcasting creates opportunities as well as dangers for the development of public service broadcasting. The danger is that broadcasting will become more standardised, right-wing and uniform; the opportunity implicit in the expansion in the number of outlets is that it will provide a wider diversity of programmes which will reflect more adequately the variety of experiences, perspectives and tastes in British society.

There is another reason why the broadcasting section of this book has a particular significance. The entire history of broadcasting in Britain (with the exception of the introduction of BBC2) has been shaped by Conservative administrations. The setting up of the BBC, the introduction of ITV, the establishment of commercial radio, the introduction of Channel 4, the development of cable TV, and now the introduction of national commercial radio, the expansion of community radio, and the introduction of voluntary quotas in the BBC and ITV for independent productions, were all implemented by governments of the Right. Even though the Labour party has been in power for 16 years in the post-war period, it has left hardly any imprint on the broadcasting system.

This is partly because the Left has paid so little attention to broadcasting, and to thinking through its ideas in strategic, policy form. The one notable exception to this — the sustained campaign for Channel 4 — has been a notable success, although it was implemented ironically by a right-wing government.

While the expansion of broadcasting creates opportunities as well as dangers, the prospect for reform in the press is receding. This is partly because a large number of people became convinced during the mid-1980s that the shortcomings of the press would be eased or solved by the introduction of new print technology. Thus, Ian Aitken, the distinguished political editor of the *Guardian*, argued shortly before Murdoch's move to Wapping, that only the intransigence of some in the print unions prevented the emergence of 'entirely new newspapers representing all points of view'. The defeat of the print unions was hailed by some as the beginning of a new break-through. 'Murdoch may have done more for the freedom of the press', enthused Bill Rodgers, then Vice-President of the Social Democratic party, 'than a dozen Royal Commissions'.

In reality, the hope that the introduction of computerised typesetting would make it much easier and cheaper to start new papers was founded on the false assumption that overpaid production workers accounted for the major part of newspaper costs. In fact, production wages only accounted for 21 per cent of Fleet Street's costs before the introduction of new technology. Consequently, the shedding of a large number of printers has not fundamentally changed the economics of publishing.

It still requires massive resources to establish a mainstream national paper. Eddie Shah spent £22.5 million on the *Star* and *Sunday Star* before running out of money; Maxwell lost over £30 million on the *London Daily News*; the *Independent* has so far spent £18 million; the *News on Sunday* burned up over £7 million. These high entry costs ensure that only those points of view which are bankrolled with a large amount of capital can be properly heard.

The actual effect of new technology in extending editorial diversity has been limited. The one unqualified gain, the *Independent*, merely serves to widen the choice of the one section of the public which is already relatively well served because it generates a large advertising subsidy. *Today* has fallen into the lap of the press's leading monopolist, Rupert Murdoch, while *Sunday Sport* adds only one new dimension — soft porn in colour. *Sunday Today*, *News on Sunday* and the *London Daily News* have folded.

The chances of exciting new national papers being established in the future is rapidly diminishing. National newspapers are using their reduced labour costs to increase the number of papers they publish and keep their prices low. This is having the effect of forcing up the run-in costs of new papers. They must publish more pages if they are not to appear thin and poor value for money, and they are forced to come in at a low price. The benefits of new technology in facilitating new launches is thus being steadily eroded.

It will be some time before the misleading prospectus accompanying the public mobilisation against print workers will be rumbled, and it becomes fully apparent that the character of the press has been little altered by the crushing of the print unions. But in the meantime, attention needs to be given to formulating the best possible way of making the press more diverse and less dominated by a few millionaires. This whole issue is very well covered in this book.

But there is one worthwhile reform (in addition to the reform of the Official Secrets Act) which it may be possible to achieve in the reasonably near future. A legal right of reply could be introduced which would give the victims of factual misrepresentation the opportunity to secure a correction published in the offending paper. The excesses of some papers, and the failure of the Press Council to curb these on a voluntary basis, has created considerable all party support for new legislation. Much of the credit for this goes to Frank Allaun, who first proposed a right of reply bill in the Commons and very effectively mobilised public support for reform.

Powerful support could also be mobilised for two other reforms — a Freedom of Information Act for which much groundwork has already been done, and for effective curbs on the concentration of media ownership. There exists already considerable concern about the way in which Rupert Murdoch has acquired a global media empire on a scale unprecedented in the history of mass communications; dismay at the way in which Murdoch's rise has contributed to a general lowering of journalistic standards in the tabloid press; and, among specialists at least, growing alarm that new communications technology could assist Murdoch, and others like him, to consolidate their domination of communications. How we should respond to this situation is perhaps the single most important question we need to confront, and is rightly a major focus of this book.

This book is the product of an unusual combination of skills and experience. Frank Allaun was for many years a distinguished politician who made reform of the media one of his principal concerns and, before that, was a successful newspaper journalist.

James Curran
March 1988

Introduction

Our country is in the middle of a media revolution. The newspaper industry has been turned upside down by the long awaited arrival of electronic printing. The structure of television in Britain is threatened by the advent of satellite and cable broadcasting. Even radio is expanding into new areas of programming.

As this revolution has gathered pace, a more unwelcome development has also occurred in the media. There has been a serious decline in professional standards of journalism over the last ten years. There is more sensationalism, less investigation; more entertainment, less explanation. This lowering of standards has coincided with new proprietors, some from overseas, buying their way into the British media. It has occurred at a time when the independence of the BBC has come under threat from a government which is happy to censor programmes and starve the Corporation of funds. And it is happening as the world's media giants are poised to consolidate further their dominant positions by exploiting satellite broadcasting.

The implication of all these developments is crucial to the long term future of a media industry which should be performing one of the most vital tasks in any democracy — keeping people informed. Other European governments have long recognised the threat, and taken positive action to preserve the editorial independence of their media. In Britain that basic freedom is at risk.

For decades there has been talk of reforming the media, but nothing significant has ever been done. Yet that has never been more important than it is today. This book is an attempt to make people realise the importance of reform — before it is too late. It is aimed at those people who already accept that there is a need for reform. It looks at the measures which have been proposed in the past, the experience of other governments overseas and puts forward a plan of action for the next government to follow.

Of course, anybody who wants to reform the media comes under immediate attack from the Press and elsewhere. You are accused of trying to bring the industry under state control; of censoring opinions and preventing debate.

This is nonsense. Nobody wants a media which is controlled by the government, but neither do we want a media which is controlled solely by commercial interests. Partisan views should be allowed to flourish, but the 'right to know' is far too valuable to be left in the hands of people who are interested primarily in profits and personal ambition. The economics of the market place is not necessarily the best structure on which to build one of the key corner-stones of a political democracy. There is a need to come up with reforms which will create the right conditions in which a free and varied media can flourish.

It is important that the current technological revolution in the media is used as a means to further that diversity — rather than burning itself out by seeking the biggest audience and slowly drifting into meaningless mediocrity.

*   *   *   *

We start our debate on a cold February day in 1976, when a gathering of distinguished academics, politicians and businessmen sat down to listen to one of the country's most highly respected newspapermen, Sir Denis Hamilton, then chairman of Times Newspapers. The occasion was the Haldane Memorial Lecture and Sir Denis was asking the question — "Who is to own the British Press ?"

Protected from the cold outside, Sir Denis warmed to his subject. "The editor is no longer a creature of the proprietor" he said. "The days of the domineering proprietor are over. Autocracy is out of fashion."

Sir Denis, of course, was lucky to be working for the newspaper empire owned by Roy Thomson, a proprietor who kept to an honourable creed. It stated quite simply:

> "I can state with the utmost emphasis that no person or group can buy or influence editorial support from any newspaper in the Thomson Group. I do not believe that a newspaper can be run properly unless its editorial columns are run freely and independently by a highly skilled and dedicated professional journalist. That is, and will continue to be my policy."

His proprietorship spawned the golden years of the *Sunday Times* under the editorship of Harold Evans. The paper's Insight Team exposed many scandals, including the Savundra insurance swindle and the Thalidomide tragedy. It lifted the role of investigative journalism away from the antics of naughty vicars, and into areas of real substance and significance for the paper's readers.

Other newspaper empires, like Mirror Group newspapers, followed Thomson's example. The board of MGN were too busy making money to interfere with the broad policy of their newspapers. But any enterprise run as a business is always susceptible to a good offer. A few months after Hamilton gave his lecture, Roy Thomson died. His son, Kenneth, took over the Thomson organisation, but after a few years of uncommitted struggle with the loss-making Times Newspapers, he sold them to the highest bidder.

This is when Sir Denis Hamilton had cause to rue his words. Six years after saying that the days of the autocratic proprietors were over, he himself was the victim of one. Shortly before Christmas in 1981 he 'resigned' as chairman of Times Newspapers. His place was taken by Rupert Murdoch, now well established as the most influential media proprietor in the Western world.

Many view this as the turning point for the British media as a whole: Murdoch's arrival on the scene coincided with major developments in technology which opened up the world of television to new owners. The autocratic proprietors have returned to be well placed to expand into every corner of the media.

Many people thought that Lord Beaverbrook's much vaunted belief that he ran the Express newspapers "purely for the purposes of making propaganda" was more appropriate in 1948 than it is now. But in the Press industry the last ten years have seen the replacement of relatively anonymous managing directors with new proprietors, eager to exert their influence: Rupert Murdoch of the *Sun*, the *News of the World*, *Today*, the *Times* and the *Sunday Times*; David Stevens of the *Daily Express*, the *Star* and the *Sunday Express*; Conrad Black of the *Daily* and *Sunday Telegraph*; and Robert Maxwell of the *Daily Mirror*, *Sunday Mirror*, the *People* and the *Scottish Daily Record* and *Sunday Mail*.

In addition to the *Daily Mail*, owned by Viscount Harmsworth of the Rothermere family, nearly all of the British Press is owned by these men. The daily reading of about thirty million people is decided by five owners.

Neither has it been easy to join the club. Eddie Shah, who was seen by many to be the prime example of how new technology would spread the ownership of newspapers, was taken over by Rupert Murdoch after sinking around thirty million pounds into his project, *Today*. The board of *News On Sunday*, the radical newcomer, had to sell out to millionaire Owen Oyston who himself was eager to join the ranks of proprietors. But he too found the going too rough, and eventually closed the venture. Now it is reported that Murdoch is eyeing up the *Financial Times*, one of the few newspapers still in independent hands.

There is one success story, however. The *Independent*, started by three financial journalists, has taken advantage of lower cost margins in electronic printing and built a steady circulation. It makes a small profit, but exists in the precarious world of newspaper economics where a rise in the price of newsprint can suddenly take a newspaper's budget into the red. There is no safety net of corporate backing if times do get rough for the *Independent*. And despite the considerable achievement of launching the newspaper, it has done little to balance the huge disproportion of newspapers committed to one ideological viewpoint. Its journalism is accurate and polished, its coverage of foreign affairs is extensive, its features touch on controversial issues.

But apart from its commendable attack on the Official Secrets Act, its editorials show that its politics are firmly of the centre.

Like the *Daily Telegraph*, the *Independent* has an important role in providing a view of the world as seen by the consensus. The *Telegraph* leans to the right of the consensus: the *Guardian* leans to the left. But as a whole, their combined two million circulation, does little to dent the combined 14 million circulation of the big five proprietors. It has also done little to stop the drift of popular newspapers, which culminated in the *Daily Star* becoming a semi-pornographic daily for a while. It published titillating stories about child abuse, while asking its readers if they would encourage their own young daughters to strip off for the paper's so called 'glamour' photographs.

It is changes like this which led Lord Cudlipp, one of Fleet Street's most respected former journalists, to say:

> "Things have happened in newspapers in the past ten years which have brought their standing in the eyes of the public to zero. The standing of journalists is lower even than politicians."

His views are backed up by a recent Marplan poll. It showed that nearly 30% of people have a low regard for journalists, and the same number of people say that their regard for journalists has decreased over the last ten years.

The importance of the media of course is that it lies at the centre of any proper democracy. When we go to a polling station to vote, we are basing our decision on information; some of it received from friends and neighbours, but most of it comes from the media — newspapers, radio and television. Thus to have a true democracy we must be able to see and appreciate a wide variety of different views and understand a series of complex facts. The problem for many people in this country is that the media only gives some of the views and some of the facts. It is like trying to pick a football team when you have only seen half the squad play.

Criticism of the media comes from a variety of sources. Women argue it presents a male perspective of the world, black people say it presents society as being almost wholly white, and minority groups, like gays, say it does not understand them. All these are important criticisms, but it is in the political arena where the most trenchant accusations are made. The peace movement, trade unions and the Labour Party all argue their case has often been badly misrepresented by the media. Analysis of the coverage of the 1985 coal dispute and the peace protest by women at Greenham Common lends support to these conclusions. Support also came from the last Royal Commission on the Press which agreed that the Labour Party had a serious disproportion of newspapers hostile to its policies compared to the number of people who supported it.

Experience has already shown that none of the social or political criticisms of the Press are likely to be solved by the technological innovations in the newspaper industry. They will make newspapers better to look at, and cheaper to run. But they are unlikely to open up significant new opportunities in the influential daily Press for newspapers which do not already fit the existing mould.

Maybe we should not be concerned with newspapers. After all it is now accepted that the majority of people turn first to television as their main source of news. But people should not under-estimate the way that the partisan headlines of the Press actually provide the raw material for the more balanced news on television.

Go into any radio or television newsroom first thing in the morning and you will see a sea of heads buried in newspapers. They are not being read for idle interest; it is part of the most important time of the day, planning the events which will be seen on the television screens that evening. Many of the items will be culled from the morning newspapers, and in that way the Press actually has a big influence in setting the agenda for the rest of the news media. Many of the worst excesses of television reporting have been initiated in newspapers. For instance, when television reports that a "row has broken out" it is often because a newspaper has set two opposing opinions against each other and created a story from them.

The majority of people perceive that they get their news from television, but it is often newspapers which are reinforcing their prejudices. Television just helps that process. This is not to say that television and radio should be ignored. Indeed several studies by researchers have concluded that the apparent neutrality of television news is a sham. The selection of pictures, topics and language is every bit as biased or misleading as the partisan headlines of the popular newspapers — the process is just more subtle. At the same time, the growth of satellite and cable could threaten the journalistic integrity of news and the quality of other programmes.

Both newspapers and broadcasting are going through processes of great change. Full colour newspapers and dish-aerials in the front garden will give the illusion that the media is set for an exciting future. It could be a false dawn. The technology may be new, but the problems of freedom of expression are as old as the spoken word.

CHAPTER ONE

The Press

"I'm with you on the free Press: It's the the newspapers I can't stand."
Tom Stoppard

A newspaper proprietor has only one vote, as has every other British citizen. But he controls newspapers with millions of readers, newspapers produced by experts, entering the home every morning or evening of life. He may also have substantial interests in local television or radio stations. He may only have one vote, but he has the power to influence the votes of millions of others.

It is not surprising that to date the first target for reform has always been the way the media is owned and controlled. It doesn't automatically solve the problems but it can create the conditions in which they can be tackled. Newspapers, radio and television, like other industries, have become concentrated in fewer and fewer hands over the years. It may be acceptable for one or two people to control the margarine factories, but is it acceptable for one or two people to dominate our way of thinking?

For example, listen to Sherlock Holmes in the Conan Doyle story, 'The Blue Carbuncle'

> "Here you are Petersen. Run down to the advertising agency, and have this put in the evening newspapers."
> "In which, sir ?"
> "Oh, in the *Globe*, *Star*, *Pall Mall*, *St James Gazette*, *Evening News*, *Standard*, *Echo*, and others that occur to you."

Today, Petersen would find not nine evening newspapers in London, as there used to be, but one — the *Standard*. Despite a brief flurry in 1987 when the *London Daily News* was launched to compete against the *Standard*, it is thought that the capital is unable to sustain more than one evening newspaper.

In the rest of the country, there is the same story. Newspapers have closed and amalgamated, and now only Belfast has more than one daily regional newspaper. In Birmingham, there is now a free morning newspaper which competes against the *Post*. But there is little investment in editorial, and the *Daily News*, as it is called, is aimed very much at the bottom of the market. The worry for many provincial newspaper groups is that other companies will want to start similar s, putting existing papers in jeopardy and reducing the value of proper journalism.

On the national scene, there are now no more than five groups which own nine out of every ten newspapers on sale. They also own long chains of provincial weeklies and evenings.

Between 1958 and 1976 seven multi-national companies bought no fewer than 552 British papers and magazines with total circulations of 49 million. The companies had interests ranging from banks and mining, to airlines and North Sea Oil.

At the head of each group is one individual. Half a dozen of these individuals virtually control the Press, and influence television and radio. One of them is *Rupert Murdoch*.

Rupert Murdoch is now the world's foremost 'media mogul'. In the past this title has gone to such people as the American tycoon, Randolph Hearst, who inspired the film 'Citizen Kane'. Mr Murdoch is somewhat less awesome than Orson Welles in the title role, but his empire spreads much wider. He was at university in Britain, but returned to his native Australia to inherit an interest in a small newspaper chain. Within a few years he had made a big enough success to start bidding for newspapers in the British market. First he bought the *News of the World*, then the former left wing newspaper, the *Sun*. This had been relaunched by the owners of the *Mirror* to replace the socialist *Daily Herald*, which had collapsed with a respectable circulation, but too little advertising. The new *Sun* had been a failure, and the owners of the *Mirror* sold it off for a song to Murdoch. As Randolph Hearst had said: "No-one ever went bust underestimating public taste." Mr Murdoch certainly didn't. Within years the *Sun* had overtaken the circulation of the *Mirror* with a steady diet of pin-ups, sensationalism, and trivia. A large part of the British public seemed to love it.

Next on the shopping list were the *Times* and the *Sunday Times*. Their Canadian owner, Kenneth Thomson, was selling them off after a long dispute which had stopped their publication for several months.

More recently, Murdoch has bought the ailing *Today* newspaper, formerly owned by Eddie Shah. In the meantime, he has built up a substantial holding in the American newspaper market to add to his interests in Australia and Britain. In addition he has shareholdings in television networks, cable television and a substantial interest in the expanding world of satellite television.

In 1986 Rupert Murdoch brought the technological revolution into Fleet Street with a big bang. Or rather, he didn't. He actually took his printing away from the centre of London to Wapping in East London, sacking over five thousand printers and employing workers from the electricians' unions to do the work. In a matter of hours, he had broken up Fleet Street as we knew it, and set a new economic agenda for newspaper publishing.

Up to that point only provincial newspapers and some national publications had patiently negotiated innovations to the production process. Pioneered in the United States, the new system means that journalists can type their stories straight onto computers, which automatically set them into type which is then laid out and printed on high-speed electronic presses situated anywhere in the country. Known as 'direct-input', it means that the job can be performed with fewer workers, and the responsibilities for one set of skilled printers, compositors, is almost eliminated. This obviously was the stumbling block to the speedy introduction of the process in this country, given that unions in Britain tended to be stronger than those in the United States. But the main unions — the National Graphical Association (NGA), the Society of Graphical and Allied Trades (SOGAT 82), and the National Union of Journalists — *had begun* to adopt a joint approach and negotiate proper deals. Important worries on the use of visual display units had been incorporated into agreements, so that workers could have set time breaks away from the screens, pregnant journalists would not have to work at the screen, and the companies would take responsibility for eye tests and special glasses.

All these carefully worked-out agreements were ignored when Rupert Murdoch decided to impose his own brand of working conditions on his employees. Spurred on by the impending launch of Eddie Shah's new colour paper, *Today*, he used the Conservative government's anti-trade union legislation to break with Fleet Street and move his four newspapers to a heavily fortified plant in Wapping. On Friday night executives were rushing through the old buildings emptying papers into packing cases: twenty four hours later the two Sunday papers were being printed in the new plant. The only problem was that he had left almost five thousand printers behind in Fleet Street, sacked without redundancy pay, though eventually he did agree to pay something.

Murdoch had told the printers that the preparations being made at Wapping were to launch a new London evening newspaper. This has never materialised. Murdoch's action led to the picketing of the Wapping plant, and large demonstrations to try to prevent the delivery lorries leaving the plant. The sight of riot police on horses charging demonstrators brought back memories of the Miners' Strike, and led to allegations that the Government were collaborating with Murdoch to break the print unions.

It is now acceptable wisdom to say that the print unions brought it upon themselves, that they had become 'Luddite' in their approach to new technology, that they insisted on inefficient manning levels, and that they earned so much anyway it did not really matter. It is true that some practices had built up which are difficult to defend to an outsider. It is also true that many printers were well paid, but that is not a crime for a skilled job. What was rarely said, however, and needs to be stressed in any history of Fleet Street, was that these practices were accepted by generations of proprietors whose poor management had actually encouraged their development. As the former editor of the *Daily Telegraph* has said:

"We are leaving behind not just history and tradition, but a nightmare almost entirely of our own making"

Lord Deedes

Management for decades had allowed intricate practices to grow up rather than risk losing the publication of their papers. Once one agreement was in place it was obvious that it would become the benchmark for any future agreements. The print unions for their part were reluctant to accept new technology unconditionally, because it would then face their members with large-scale redundancy.

Mr Murdoch's battle of Wapping effectively led to the end of Fleet Street. New plants have been built on the Isle of Dogs, and offices have moved all over London. Not one national newspaper intends to stay in Fleet Street.

In Britain, Murdoch's papers are now highly profitable. And they need to be, because he has sights on a larger slice of the world's media cake. His British profits are said to be financing an astonishing expansion into television companies and the growing world market in satellite programming. He has also set his sights on a larger share of the television market in Britain.

For the moment both the BBC and ITV is 'regulated', and is protected from the preying eyes of media moguls. But he has consistently run a major campaign through his newspapers advocating the break-up of the BBC. Columns in the *Sunday Times* have been devoted to putting his case before the Peacock Committee, which was set up to investigate the Corporation's future. Then the *Sun* and the *Sunday Times* turned on the independent companies in ITV, accusing them of waste and extravagance.

His newspapers have also worked hard to put political pressure on both the BBC and ITV. It was Murdoch's *Sunday Times* which created the story which eventually led to the banning of the BBC documentary on Northern Ireland (*Real Lives*) by the then Home Secretary, Leon Brittan.

The papers' attacks on the existing broadcasting set-up (which is highly praised throughout the world), has nothing to with concern about the viewers. The hope is that they will lead to its break-up and provide new opportunities to add to Murdoch's television empire. Already he owns Sky Channel, Europe's popular English-speaking satellite station. The deregulation of the BBC, and the break-up of ITV, would allow him to buy his way into new areas of programme making and exert more control over the country's media.

A concentration of the media leads to a concentration of views. In a democratic society many people regard this as an development for the free expression of public opinion.

Murdoch has wasted no time in making sure that his newspapers reflect his view of the world. In an ideal society it is healthy that individual views are expressed, but where the opportunity to present one's opinion is based upon the concentration of wealth, it deprives a lot of people from having a say.

Even if we say that papers like the *Sun* have every right to be partisan, there is no excuse for telling lies. The *Sun* has the worst track record of any newspaper for blatant inaccuracy, often used in a highly political way. Two simple examples; the case of Mrs Marica McKay and the libel settlement of Graham Gooch, the England cricketer.

Mrs McKay is the widow of the Falklands hero, Sergeant McKay, one of two winners of the Victoria Cross during the conflict. At the time he was awarded the medal, the *Sun* carried an 'exclusive' story with Mrs McKay about her intimate thoughts, including a statement that her husband had had an intimation of his death.

The entire story had been made up. She never talked to the *Sun* and the story about her husband's foresight of death was false. The Press Council criticised the newspaper heavily for the fabrication of the story. But this has not stopped them from continuing to print falsehoods and inaccuracy.

Another story was on the England cricketer, Graham Gooch. The *Sun* carried a story which alleged that the batsman "could not care less" about the England team losing in Australia because he had been banned from playing for his country since he joined a tour in South Africa. The story was even marked as an 'exclusive'. It was so exclusive that even Graham Gooch had never heard of it. He had never spoken to the *Sun*, and the entire interview had been invented. Gooch won £25,000 in libel damages and costs. He was lucky. There is no legal aid for libel, and most people do not have the money to take rich newspapers to court.

In 1987, the number of adjudicated complaints to the Press Council rose by 50%. Two of Murdoch's papers were well in front as having the most judgements against them: the *Sun* led the daily newspaper league; the *News of The World* was in front among the Sundays.

The record of the *Sun* has obviously not concerned the Conservative government. For such services to journalism, the former editor of the *Sun*, Larry Lamb, was awarded a knighthood by Margaret Thatcher. Murdoch himself is reported to have an antipathy towards honours. In 1976 he told the New York Village *Voice* that he had been offered a knighthood "a few times", but turned them down. In fact, of course, as he is not a British citizen, he could only get an honorary knighthood anyway. He changed his nationality from Australian to American in order to get around US laws on the media.

Of course, the British establishment does not reward newspaper proprietors for being great communicators; it rewards them with such honours because they have the power to control public opinion and set the agenda for radio and television coverage of news. The *Sun* has a circulation of over four million, which suggests a readership of over ten million.

Its power to influence public opinion is immense. During May 1984 a survey showed that the paper daily carried a front page headline or a story attacking the Coal dispute and ten million readers were left in no doubt as to whom they should support.

In 1986 the *Sun* was continuing its campaign, shared with other newspapers of the right, in attacking inner city Labour councils. In order to dress up these attacks they resorted to fictional and highly improbable stories. For instance they claimed that Hackney Council had banned the use of the word 'man-hole', because it was considered sexist. It was untrue. The council had never debated the use of the word, had never issued any instruction on it, and one of the men quoted in the story as being an employee of the council did not appear on their pay-roll.

Again in 1986, an equally improbable story emerged among the right wing press. This time it was claimed that black bin-liners were to be banned in Haringey because they were racist. Once again there was not a shred of truth to the story. The source of the story was quoted as being 'anonymous', and the very next day, the Civic Services Committee of the council went ahead as planned and accepted a tender from a local supplier for black bin-liners.

But though supporters of the Labour movement may be driven into apoplexy by some of the stories in the *Sun* it should be remembered that many working people and Labour voters buy the *Sun* by choice. They may not agree with the politics, but there is obviously something in the newspaper they enjoy. It is not good enough, and is condescending, to say the paper merely 'panders to the lowest common denominator'. It is also interesting to note that opinion polls show that over 30% of the readers of the *Sun* think it supports the Labour Party !

Certainly the issues that the *Sun* constantly raises — sex, war and hanging — produce gut reactions, whereas stories about health cuts, nuclear disarmament and local government, take a little more thought to raise emotions. But the human basis of such stories exists in both camps. It is just that the majority of the Press are not willing to highlight the victims of unemployment, the problems of nurses or what many see as the courage of the women at Greenham Common. If, and when, conditions exist in which a free press can highlight such stories, it should be remembered that left-thinking newspapers are going to have to present themselves as well, or better, than the well produced right-wing newspapers like the *Sun* and the *Daily Mail*.

There is of course, the *Daily Mirror*. Doesn't its existence refute all the arguments for reform of the Press? It does have a huge circulation, along with the Scottish papers and the *People* and the *Sunday Mirror*, and it has urged its readers to vote Labour at each General Election.

In only a few years, the *Mirror's* proprietor, Robert Maxwell, has risen from the comparative obscurity of being a book publisher, to rivalling Murdoch as Britain's top media tycoon. He owns the *Daily Mirror*, the *Sunday Mirror*, the *Scottish Daily Record* and the *Scottish Sunday Mail*. He launched the unsuccessful *London Daily News*. He also owns stakes in television, and has control of a European satellite station. The only qualification he has for controlling such a huge segment of our media is that he is an extremely rich man.

Once a Labour MP, Maxwell announced he would continue to support the Party as long as "it keeps Tony Benn out of the saddle". He thus sets conditions on maintaining the slender support which exists in the Press for the Labour Party. Only a year after the takeover of Mirror Group newspapers it was reported that the newspaper group would officially no longer be exclusive supporters of the Party. Maxwell's support at future elections will clearly have to be bought or sold on the political manifesto. And though the *Mirror* gave whole-hearted support to Labour in the 1987 General Election, it is clear that Maxwell has the power to exert considerable influence over the Labour Party, even though he has no formal position, and has not been elected to any of its committees.

The takeover of the *Mirror* gives us a classic illustration of the low regard we accord to the freedom of the press in Britain. The *Mirror's* parent company — Reed International — had promised not to sell to any one individual. Nobody was to own more than 15% of the shares. Clive Thornton, the managing director, was preparing ambitious plans to let the group's employees gain substantial holdings in the company. Other proposals included a new Sunday paper, as well as a new evening newspaper for London.

While Thornton was telling *Mirror* workers in Manchester about their plans, he heard that Maxwell had put in a bid. At first it was rejected, but Maxwell increased his offer. Sir Alexander Jarratt, chairman of Reed International, decided to break his promise not to sell it to an individual buyer, and accepted Maxwell's offer of £107 million. Reed's commitment to freedom of the press was as thin as the chance of winning million pound bingo. Within weeks, Clive Thornton had gone, and the building in Manchester where he first learnt the news had been officially re-christened 'Maxwell House'.

But Maxwell isn't the first proprietor of the *Mirror* to play the role of unelected power broker in the Labour Party. The paper has consistently tried to control the labour movement rather than reflect it. Since the last war it has employed three main themes.

It has angered trade unionists by its criticism of some union activities. They believe its criticism is not constructive, which would be perfectly proper, but actually undermines many of the things that the unions exist to protect.

The second issue is nuclear disarmament. Over the years CND has been continually opposed by the *Mirror*, along with the current Labour policy on disarmament. It was the *Daily Mirror* who described the chair of CND as "The chairman of CND, Mrs Joan Ruddock, a beautifully intact lady of 38, with model's legs and a great amount of femininity..." Other male leaders of CND have never received such insulting treatment.

The third issue which concerns some activists is the Common Market. This is a justifiable area of debate, and therefore worthy of such, rather than the almost fanatical support the *Mirror* has given it. This is despite the fact that many on the Left argue that EEC membership has demonstrably affected the country's well-being.

The problem for most newspaper proprietors is that as businessmen they are individually inclined towards the Right. A large percentage of people, however, vote for left of centre policies, and there is a huge market to be tapped. The owners of the *Mirror* realise this, and so for a time, did Express Newspapers when it launched the *Daily Star*. At the time of the 1983 election, the *Daily Star* had built up a working class readership mostly in the North. It had often campaigned on behalf of Labour policies, and by all accounts was a supporter of the Labour Party. But in the General Election this marketing ploy was put to the test, and of course the political reality of ownership came into force. After years of support for the Labour Party, the day of the General Election dawned with a front page headline of "Sorry, Michael. We cannot vote for you." Alongside it was an unflattering full page photograph of the Labour leader, Michael Foot, with donkey jacket and walking stick, taken several months earlier.

The *Star*, of course, has gone through many changes since then. It is of course one of the titles of Express Newspapers, which has itself seen some changes over the years. Its newest owner is *David Stevens*, the chairman of United Newspapers. He won a takeover battle with the previous owners — Fleet Holdings — to have the privilege of running the *Daily Express*, the *Sunday Express*, and the *Star*. United Newspapers already owned 70 provincial newspapers in Britain, Link House magazines and a large chain of other newspapers. In America it owned Newswire, a satellite based communications network, and a successful magazine chain. The *Express* and the *Star* are strident supporters of the Conservative Party.

The previous owner, Lord 'Vic' Matthews, was also a staunch supporter of the Conservative Party. His own company, Trafalgar House, is one of the biggest contributors to Conservative Party funds, as well as other right wing groups like the Economic League. Lord Matthews, however, believed in a form of editorial independence. He is reputed to have said that his editors will have complete freedom "as long as they agree with the policy I have laid down."

His policy included strong support for nuclear weapons, which sometimes verged on the obsessive. The *Daily Express* was particularly interested in the women of Greenham Common who had set up camp outside the airbase to protest at the arrival of Cruise missiles in Britain. One of the paper's ploys was to send in a reporter posing as a peace campaigner to discredit those at the camp. It was billed as the "compelling story of Sarah Bond, *Express* undercover girl, who posed as a peace woman at the world's most notorious peace protest camp. " Much of it was devoted to cheap lesbian innuendo in a story entitled "Life and Love in the Camp that Bans Men."

Their attempts to smear the Greenham women led to two complaints upheld by the Press Council. One of the stories told of how the Greenham women had formed a barricade against a secret delivery of missile casings. As it happened, such an event would have been entirely consistent, but on this occasion it never actually happened. The Ministry of Defence, the Thames Valley Chief Constable, and Newbury District Council all had no record of the incidents described.

The paper was then censured over another Greenham Common story. They claimed that areas near the camp had become polluted by the women's presence, implying a serious danger to health. However, when the Press Council questioned the local Director of Environmental Health, he said there was no danger to health at all. During this time there was also a spate of stories which whipped up hysteria among the local residents about the presence of the Greenham Common women. It never seemed to occur to the newspapers involved to ask residents their views about the fact that Greenham Common had now become a major target in the event of a nuclear war.

But none of the censures from the Press Council have distracted the *Daily Express* from continuing its campaign against the women at Greenham. Downing Street was not unobservant, and before long Vic Matthews had become Lord Matthews. Since then, the *Express* has continued in its support for the Conservatives, and David Stevens has followed the previous proprietor and risen to the ranks of the Lords.

The *Express*, of course, was once owned by perhaps the greatest of all press barons, Lord Beaverbrook. He told the 1947 Royal Commission on the Press that he ran the newspaper "purely for the purposes of making propaganda." He was being honest, but the politics of the *Express* in those days were far more open than similar papers nowadays when columnists like Michael Foot and James Cameron graced its pages.

Take the *Daily Mail* and the *Mail on Sunday* for instance. They too go back to a great press baron, in this case, Lord Northcliffe, the pioneer of popular newspapers. His descendant, Lord Rothermere, now controls the parent company, Associated Newspapers, which also owns the London evening paper, the *Standard*, countless provincial newspapers and extensive holdings in television and radio.

In many ways it is a classic example of how to do political journalism well. It has none of the crude sloganising of the *Sun*. It lures the reader by having a brilliantly compact lay-out, well written human interest tales and strong angles for running stories. Its overt political coverage comes on its leader pages, where anything further left than a Tory 'wet' is treated with the scorn normally given to mass murderers and rapists. Yet apart from the obvious diatribes of Andrew Alexander and Paul Johnson, politics are also presented in the selection of stories and the way that the news is written.

Most of this is a tribute to Sir David English, the man who became editor when it went tabloid, and skilfully produced a newspaper which though subtler than the *Sun*, is probably more effective in its support for Margaret Thatcher. He too was the recipient of an honour from Margaret Thatcher, but as a mere editor, he only became *Sir* David English.

Another Fleet Street personality with a long pedigree is *Lord Hartwell*, until recently proprietor of the *Daily Telegraph* and the *Sunday Telegraph*. He relinquished overall control of the family group of newspapers to a foreign buyer, Conrad Black, a Canadian financier. Lord Hartwell is a descendant of the less well known press baron, Lord Kemsley.

Under Hartwell, the newspapers built up a strong reputation. They support the Conservative Party, but do it in a way that is consistent with the standards of proper journalism. Its extensive news coverage, and its contacts within the Conservative Party, have made it an essential read for those who want to keep up with political developments in Britain. As one former Labour Minister said recently, "You know where you are with the *Telegraph*". It is both partisan and responsible. And as the left wing Labour MP, Dennis Skinner, says "It's got a good crossword." In contrast, it has been said that the *Times* under Murdoch no longer gives either a feeling of independence, or a feeling of political impartiality. To many, its views seem to reflect the whim of the publisher. Readers now no longer know whether stories have been selected for their news value, or for political reasons.

The newspapers we have mentioned so far control over ninety per cent of the British Press. The five men who run them have the power to influence the minds of tens of millions of people. The remainder have a smaller proportion of the market, but can have influence in certain areas. The *Financial Times*, owned by *Pearson and Sons* is essential reading for Treasury officials, City businessmen, company secretaries and trade union officials. The *Guardian*, owned by the *Scott Trust* is read largely by the liberal middle class. The *Observer*, owned by *'Tiny' Rowlands* of Lonrho, is a well respected, but poorly funded rival to the other Sunday papers.

Newcomers to this stable of publications include the successful

Independent, the unsuccessful *News On Sunday*, and the *Today* newspaper, which nearly went bankrupt and was taken over by Rupert Murdoch.

These newcomers were welcome in a pattern of newspaper publishing which had gradually shrunk over the years. It is hoped that the advent of new technology will have the lasting power to upset this pattern. Our experience so far, with the exception of the *Independent*, is not encouraging. Eddie Shah, who had set out to break the mould by breaking the unions, found himself once again the owner of a small provincial group of newspapers. It was Shah, fresh from his dispute in Warrington with the print unions, who raised the capital to set up an entirely new form of newspaper publishing in Britain. Journalists would have 'direct input' into the production process, thus getting rid of compositors; printers would be replaced by members of the electricians unions. His paper, *Today*, would be the first all colour paper in Britain, be politically aligned to the Alliance, and aimed at the same market as the *Mail* and the *Express*. But he launched before he was ready. There were problems with the colour printing, and the paper seemed uncertain of where to pitch itself editorially. Without the back-up of a large corporation, Eddie Shah had to sell the paper to survive. In the end, his catalytic breakthrough in new technology was borrowed by the other existing proprietors, and his paper was bought by Rupert Murdoch.

Market Share of the Press

PROPRIETOR	NEWSPAPERS	CIRCULATION (Dec 87)
Lord Stevens	*Daily Express*	1,708,000
	Daily Star	1,288,583
	Sunday Express	2,214,612
Robert Maxwell	*Daily Mirror*	3,130,000
	Daily Record	767,485
	Sunday Mirror	2,980,675
	Sunday People	2,905,693
Rupert Murdoch	*The Sun*	4,080,000
	Today	344,000
	The Times	442,375
	The Sunday Times	1,220,021
	News of the World	4,941,966
Lord Rothermere	*Daily Mail*	1,820,000
	Mail On Sunday	1,850,000
Lord Hartwell	*Daily Telegraph*	1,146,917
	Sunday Telegraph	720,902
OTHERS	*The Guardian*	493,582
	The Independent	383,315
	Financial Times	209,278
	Observer	773,514

The circulation figures show that Lord Stevens has a 19% market share of the daily figures, Maxwell has 25%, Murdoch has 31% and the others make up only 25% of the daily sales.

The other new newspaper, *News On Sunday*, had an equally rough ride, and also failed to prove that new technology can provide diversity. The story of *News On Sunday* is told later as there are important lessons to be learned by others attempting similar ventures. But at least it did throw up perhaps the most unlikely proprietor of them all. Mr Owen Oyston, who until this time had been best known for falling fully clothed into a swimming pool during a commercial for his estate agency, announced he was going to save the paper. Having sold his business for nearly 30 million pounds, he had already built up interests in local radio and cable television in the North West. A maverick figure, he lived in a mock Gothic castle with buffalo roaming the grounds. He also had a passing resemblance to General Custer, which seemed particularly appropriate as the debts mounted up, the criticism increased, and he changed his editor frequently. But in the meantime, a large number of staff had been sacked, and the paper moved inexorably from the previous highly principled idea of what *News On Sunday* was going to be about. It does show one thing: that the passion for owning newspapers often cuts across all good sense. It is an example of the sort of motivation which drives on the proprietors of our national newspapers. Commercial success often comes second to personal prestige, but both can be very dangerous for a democratic Press.

CHAPTER TWO

Television and Radio

John Logie Baird could have a lot to answer for. As the inventor of television he has transformed communications throughout the world. Its development has continued at such a pace that it has not been easy to sit back and decide whether television is a good or a bad phenomenon. Eventually it will control our lives in so many ways that it will not be possible to make a dispassionate decision on such a question.

The development of broadcasting in Britain has been more controlled than in other Western countries like America where there is a more *laissez faire* tradition. On the other hand the control over broadcasting has been infinitely less than in France, where President De Gaulle freely censored news pictures of the 1968 Paris riots on the all-government television networks. In Britain, we have a regulated broadcasting system, and an openly commercial Press. Our broadcasting has a worldwide reputation, our Press does not. Yet at the moment the trend among government thinking is to go for a de-regulated broadcasting system, similar to that in the United States, and more in keeping with the way that the Press has developed.

In Britain, we have seen the introduction of four national radio channels, four television networks, many local radio stations, and the transmission of information data onto our screens at home through services like Prestel, Ceefax and Oracle. Cable television is already underway and a new global dimension has been introduced to the future by the development of satellite broadcasting. In Britain, broadcasting is regulated; in other words it is run by publicly accountable bodies — the BBC, and by the IBA in the commercial sector. Both of them answer to supposedly independent boards of publicly appointed people. Satellite broadcasting threatens to overthrow this slowly created system of control, which successive governments until now has been found preferable to free competition.

The Government, at the time of writing, is looking at reforming broadcasting following an inquiry by Professor Alan Peacock. It is thought that both the BBC and ITV will experience changes, including the introduction of a new channel and the selling off of ITV franchises to the highest bidder. Proposals have been put forward by the Home Secretary, Douglas Hurd, to change the face of radio in Britain. Other changes are also occurring in both the BBC and ITV as a result of the introduction of Channel Four. Independent companies now have greater access onto the main networks. In this chapter we see how the structure of broadcasting has developed in this country, and highlight the areas most likely to change.

Our television has been described either as the "best television in the world", or more realistically, the "least worst television in the world". Nobody quite knows why it has achieved this reputation, but it seems to have some truth. Some say it is because our system of broadcasting has benefitted by being balanced between commercial output and public service output. The BBC has set a standard which commercial companies have been obliged to follow, and on occasions improve upon.

So how does this system of the "least worst" broadcasting work? The BBC, set up in 1926 with a Royal Charter, is now the second largest broadcasting organisation in the world. At present the BBC runs two network television channels, four radio channels, a network of local radio stations, as well as the World Service. Everything, apart from the World Service is paid for by the licence fee, which is determined by the government of the day. It is run by the Board of Governors, a selection of the "great and good", appointed by the Prime Minister through the Privy Council. These twelve people in turn appoint the Director General, who chairs the Board of Management.

The Commercial companies are run by the IBA, the Independent Broadcasting Authority. It too is awarded a licence to broadcast and has a governing body of twelve people appointed by the Home Secretary. Independent companies are awarded the franchise for running each of the fifteen regional television stations, and over fifty commercial radio stations. In addition, the IBA also oversees the Independent Television News, TV AM and Channel Four. Many of the shareholders of commercial television and radio stations have interests in other forms of media. The IBA however, discourages groups from having a controlling interest in more than one television station.

The introduction of Channel Four in 1980 solved the oft-debated question of what to do with the spare channel. Rather than allocate it to existing ITV companies, it was decided to give it an independent structure within the IBA. The companies would collect the advertising on its behalf, and the IBA would allocate it a budget each year. This was seen as the best way of protecting the new channel from the sharp end of commercial television. By having a fixed budget, there was no incentive to provide so called 'down market' programmes to increase audiences and therefore raise the amount of cash raised through advertising. Channel Four was to be put in the hands of a company board appointed by the IBA. This included the former Trade Secretary, Edmund Dell, and the film maker, Richard Attenborough.

Channel Four was not to make programmes in its own right, but to commission independent companies to provide the programmes for the new network. Under its first Chief Executive, Jeremy Isaacs, commissioning editors were appointed to select programme ideas and to provide a budget for each commission. For the first time, producers and directors outside the existing television framework were given real access to the airwaves. Channel Four money has led to the production of some impressive British films, and the range of programming has extended the scope open to viewers in Britain. The former BBC controller, Michael Grade, took over as Chief Executive in early 1988, promising to work closer with the ITV network, but to continue to maintain the range of programmes seen on Channel Four since its inception.

The Peacock Committee, set up by the Government, considered the possibility of introducing advertising to all, or just certain parts, of the BBC. It also looked to see whether it would be preferable to allow Channel Four to collect its own advertising revenue. Other proposals included selling the franchises of the ITV regions to the highest bidder, or even opening up more networks.

The possibility of introducing advertising to the BBC caused the biggest controversy. It was argued that such a move would upset the delicate balance between commercial and public service broadcasting which would lead to a corresponding drop in the quality of programmes. This in itself would remove the only weapon that the networks have in defending themselves from the long-term introduction of satellite broadcasting. After all, it is argued, the best way to stop people from flocking to watch satellite programmes is by continuing to provide a strong range of quality programming made in Britain.

The Peacock Committee was the first major study of broadcasting since Lord Annan's Royal Commission in 1977. It aroused considerable debate among those with vested interests. Rupert Murdoch used the full might of his newspaper holdings to argue his case for the break-up of the BBC and the introduction of advertising. As we have seen, Mr Murdoch stands to gain by picking up the most profitable parts of the Corporation. The overwhelming evidence to the committee from both the independent television companies and the BBC was that it would severely affect the quality of programmes in Britain. They also argued that it would threaten the financial viability of some of the smaller television companies, with the "near certainty" that many commercial local radio stations, and even newspapers would go bankrupt. Their position was hardly surprising, but it was backed up by two independent economic studies. These studies were commissioned by the committee, one from Professor Alan Budd, and one from economists at the City University Business School.

The other side of the argument mainly represented the advertising industry which believed the introduction of commercials would help the profitability of the BBC and help maintain their programme standards. The advertisers, of course, were as predictable in their submission as the commercial companies because of their hope that such a move would lead to a drop in the rates of television advertising.

Last of all there was the evidence of opinion polls which asked people if they minded having advertising on the BBC. In a MORI poll in Murdoch's *Times*, over 60% said they did not mind advertising on the BBC. Later a BBC executive said that the question was framed in such a way that "it's surprising that 100 per cent do not want an apparently free lunch." More careful analysis of the findings of another poll, this time by NOP and commissioned by Peacock, showed that four fifths say they don't mind advertising "providing the quality of programmes is not lowered." The experience of America and other commercially funded television networks suggest that some reduction in standards would almost certainly occur.

The Peacock Committee eventually came down on the side of those who did not want advertising on the BBC. But they did suggest that limited advertising might be introduced onto the popular radio networks. One of the most far-reaching recommendations was that the system of awarding the franchises to independent companies should be changed. Accordingly the next franchise 'round' has been frozen to 1992, and it is expected that some form of open tender will be introduced when the Government publishes its Broadcasting Act in 1988.

Nearly all the submissions to the Peacock Committee concentrated on the standards of programmes and the commercial implications throughout the media industry. Very few looked beyond the financial question to the problems of control in the BBC, which have become more acute in the last five years. One submission which did consider these problems was from the National Union of Journalists.

The NUJ had two fears. First, that increased pressure on ratings in order to win advertisers would lead to less emphasis on news, current affairs and local programmes. The other fear was that advertisers or sponsors could directly, or indirectly, affect programme policy. They noted the interest in the BBC of both Rupert Murdoch and Robert Maxwell and concluded that the "Government should act to strengthen public service broadcasting as the one system independent of commercial pressure and incapable of takeover by multi-media, multi-national companies." The union proposed a Broadcasting Review Board, which would recommend members for the BBC Board of Governors and the IBA, as well as doing an independent assessment of the Corporation's application for an increased licence fee. The purpose of the Board would be to add an extra buffer between the BBC and the government of the day.

The NUJ was reflecting current criticism of the existing system of funding the BBC, and claims that the Conservative Government had consistently been trying to 'gag' the Corporation. At the moment the licence fee is fixed by the government, and the BBC has to go with its 'begging bowl' to the Cabinet.

This has inevitably led to accusations that it can be politically controlled by the government of the day, whether it belongs to the present incumbent, or to someone like the Labour Prime Minister, Harold Wilson. It is generally accepted that Mr Wilson felt that his control of the licence fee was the biggest hold he had over the BBC.

Mrs Thatcher as Prime Minister took such a hold a stage further with the appointment to the Board of Governors of well known supporters of her administration. She appointed Stuart Young, the brother of Cabinet member, Lord Young, as Chairman of the Board of Governors. His appointment came under severe criticism when pressure was put on the BBC not to screen a documentary on Northern Ireland. The programme, called *Real Lives*, had not been seen either by Mrs Thatcher, or the Home Secretary, Leon Brittan, when both called upon the BBC to ban it. The Board of Governors under the Cabinet Minister's brother, Stuart Young, caved into the demands of the Government and stopped the programme from being transmitted.

The BBC's Director General, Alasdair Milne, returned from holiday, to find the decision had already been made. He finally allowed the programme to go out with minor alterations. The significance of the event however was that the normally pliant Board of Governors had decided to flex its muscles in the politically controversial field of programming.

When Stuart Young died a little while later, the Government appointed the former *Times* executive, Marmaduke Hussey, as Chairman of the BBC Governors. One of his early acts was to fire Alasdair Milne as Director General, and bring in an accountant, Michael Checkland, in his place. Now programme makers were becoming thin on the ground in the BBC's upper echelons, leaving it more vulnerable than ever before to a Board of Governors, many of whom were appointed by Mrs Thatcher. Late in 1987, John Birt, a newcomer from ITV, was brought in as Deputy Director General to run News and Current Affairs under a single directorate. Experienced journalistic heads rolled in the two departments, and the revolution was complete. Now critics say the BBC has been neutered, and that Mr Checkland's boast that the BBC is just like any other "billion pound business" is an insult to creative programme makers. The views of the critics were strengthened by two appointments in the upper administration of the BBC. First the special adviser to Lord Young, the Trade and Industry Secretary, was appointed as director of corporate affairs. Then a former Conservative parliamentary candidate was appointed to head a new policy and planning unit, which would among other tasks, "underpin the co-ordination of editorial policy and practice across the Corporation."

Current criticisms

The structure of television and radio has grown up in a far more regulated way than the Press. This is not only because television has fewer channels on offer, but it reflects a more centralist tradition in Europe as a whole. For some this means an unacceptable degree of control by government; for others it has produced a medium which is less biased and more objective than newspapers. The tone of news and current affairs on radio and television is far less strident than the partisan posturings of the popular press. Yet this so called 'objective' view can often lead to an exaggerated degree of concensus on issues which attract many opinions.

A recent public survey showed that over 70 per cent of people now see television as their primary source of news. It is partly because television and radio are capable of a quicker reaction to events, partly because the number of televisions in the country has reached saturation point, and partly because many people perceive that their news on television is untainted by the excesses of what used to be known as Fleet Street. It has long been a saying that "you should not believe anything you read in newspapers". People's reactions to television, however, reflect the power of the medium, the delusion that because the pictures on the screen illustrate the words of the presenter, it must be true.

The Glasgow Media Group, established at Glasgow University in 1974, has encouraged people to become more sophisticated in the way they view television. The Group argues that the viewer cannot, and does not, get an accurate reflection of events. The intrinsic political viewpoints of the director, producer or reporter determine the analysis within each story, however subconscious such pressures are to the people working on it. The way they select some pictures, and leave out others can drastically change the viewer's perception of the item. The editing of interviews, which gives the viewer the impression that it is unedited, can mean that your subject can win the argument in interview, but lose it in the cutting room.

On isolated occasions such bias may stem from decisions made at a higher level. The coverage of the Falklands War is a particularly drastic example of this. But in the majority of cases it is unlikely that this is caused by a conspiracy. It stems from the fact that many people who control the media have come from the educated middle class who have been taught to reflect the concensus view of the world.

For many years it was well known that the newsrooms of the BBC were full of public school and Oxbridge educated journalists, in the same way as the Civil Service was full of Classics graduates. The BBC training schemes were often almost entirely made up of graduates from Oxford and Cambridge. It has recently been revealed that they were also vetted by M15 for their political sympathies, along with other BBC programme makers. Independent television is slightly different,

34

with the regional companies having a wider spread of recruitment. But the network news comes from ITN, many of whom came from a similar privileged background to the BBC journalists, or were recruited from the BBC in the first place.

The introduction of local radio, and the expansion of regional television, means that such an elitist view of the BBC and ITV is now outdated. Such training grounds have spread their nets wider for talent and many of those people are now working in the national newsrooms. But the people in charge are still from the same upper echelons who have a distinctly concensus view of society.

The record of current affairs, documentaries and drama, has been different, often producing programmes which investigate, agitate, and criticise the *status quo*. The new breed of news programmes like Newsnight on BBC 2, and Channel Four News, have introduced more inquiring coverage of daily events. But their audience is small compared to the daily news programmes of the major channels. Our views are influenced by the careful balance of serious and funny stories, of important issues wrapped in cosy nutshells and summed up by reporters in far flung lands, of exciting pictures often taking precedence over relevant ones, and politicians giving their views on the world in 30 second bursts. It has been said that Mrs Thatcher has been trained to limit her principal point to just thirty seconds specifically to get her message across on television and radio news. Anything longer, and she knows it will be cut.

To an extent, the limitations of the concensus view of the world has already been recognised by the introduction of Channel Four, and access programmes on BBC 2 like Open Space. Alongside this, both BBC and ITV have promised greater airtime for independent companies, which could give scope for more views on both the network channels. Alternatively it could lead to the contracting out of 'uninteresting' work like quiz shows and sport, and leave the more challenging areas of drama and documentaries to be made in-house. Certainly, both the BBC and ITV companies are concerned about keeping up a certain standard. Channel Four has shown that independent companies can make some very good programmes, and some very bad ones as well.

Other developments

Radio

The main expansion of radio has been in local radio. Set up to replace the pirate radio stations in the sixties, local radio has spread across the country, so that nearly every large town or city now has a commercial or BBC local radio station. Some are more successful than others, and they vary greatly in output. Some are almost entirely pop music stations, while others, mainly BBC stations, have a large amount of all speech programmes. At their best, they cater for minority groups and provide a good community service, particularly during emergencies. At worst, they are a poor imitation of the BBC's Radio One and Two network stations.

Meanwhile new plans unveiled by the Home Secretary in January 1988 propose three new national commercial radio networks, licensed by auction to the highest bidder. These would be responsible to a new Radio Authority, separate from the BBC and the IBA. The Green Paper suggests that the Radio Authority will operate with a "light touch" allowing stations to operate under greatly relaxed regulations. It is hoped that hundreds of new stations could also be established at city, local and community level. Existing ILR stations could have the option of staying with the IBA, or moving under the wings of the new Radio Authority.

Some controls have been placed on the development of these stations however. Control will not be permitted for non-'European' nationals, no group will be permitted to own more than one network, or six local stations, and cross ownership of newspapers and radio will be restricted.

The development of this legislation is interesting as it ties in with the controversial proposals on community radio which were ditched at the eleventh hour by the Government. They had announced that 20 experimental stations would be set up which had been chosen from nearly six hundred applicants. The official aim of the experiment was to provide access for minorities like racial groups, or people with specific musical tastes. In reality, it was an attempt by the Home Office to come to terms with the demand created by the expansion of a new pirate radio network. At its best it would give racial minorities the chance to run radio for their own communities, rather than relying on individual programmes on stations catering for the white minority. Abruptly, without full explanation, the Home Secretary cancelled the experiment.

Now comes this far more radical proposal for three new networks, and the possibility of several hundred community radio stations. There are two main areas of concern. The IBA is worried that this is the first attempt to de-regulate broadcasting, and try out a system of competitive tendering for the allocation of frequencies, which could later be applied to the franchises of television regions. Others are concerned that it will affect the quality of existing local stations. They claim that the advertising cake will be split so widely that all stations will end up as "low cost units run by volunteers and freelances, on low pay without trade union recognition."

Despite these concerns, it is expected that the radio proposals will be included in the Broadcasting Act due before the end of 1988.

Cable television
The introduction of cable and satellite could have significant long-term

effects on the shape of our media. Already some homes have a choice, not just of four channels, but of over ten. In twenty years people could have several hundred channels on offer for their viewing. Nobody knows what the impact will be on the existing four networks. The introduction of the new channels to Britain is comparatively recent. Cable television was only given the go-ahead in 1983, and it was only made legal for individuals to buy their own satellite dishes in 1985.

Cable is run by the Cable Authority which has awarded franchises for selected areas on an experimental basis. It is not a recent technological breakthrough: homes in America and other parts of Europe have been cabled for some time. In many cases this was due to necessity. Physical geographical barriers, like mountains, made it impossible to transmit a strong signal to receivers in many towns. Consequently they took the costly step of piping television programmes on cables which had to be physically laid into the houses. Once there, however, the cable could carry far more than just the four channels available on airwave transmission. In Britain, transmitters could successfully cover most of the country, so cable never really became a need.

Recently, however, with the development of fibre optics, cables have, been able to carry more and more separate channels which has led to their introduction in Britain. This has not been immediately as popular as predicted. It is an expensive business to lay cables into entire homes. The new companies have found difficulties in persuading householders to take the service, and where they have, up to ten per cent have not renewed their subscriptions. It is now thought that many cable companies will not start making a profit until the 1990s. At the end of 1987, only 254,508 homes were connected, and only ten of the twenty two franchises awarded by the Cable Authority were operational.

The slow take-up of cable could reflect the relatively diverse and strong programming on the four main channels. The main impetus for cable in America, apparently, was public dissatisfaction with the similar range of game shows and situation comedies found on the networks. Where there has been dissatisfaction here, it has partly been met by the spread of video recorders, which have not taken off in the States in the same way. The video recorder is now a regular feature of many homes, giving viewers the chance to control their own television preferences.

Satellite

It is thought that satellite will be more popular than cable. At the moment, its success is linked to cable. Only a small percentage of people have bought the satellite dishes which are necessary to receive the programmes directly from space. So at the moment many of the programmes can only be seen by viewers in Britain if they subscribe to cable, and their cable company takes these channels.

This will change when the satellite dishes become smaller and cheaper. In Europe the satellite channels have already carved out a significant share of the market, particularly in areas which already have cable television. Two satellites, Intelsat and the European Communications Satellite, carry over twenty channels already, and more are planned.

The English-speaking channels have been slower to evolve, but already it can be seen that with no government regulation the people who already own the media in Britain are in a position to exploit the new market. Robert Maxwell of the *Mirror* intends to provide two channels, one for films, and one for news and entertainment. Rupert Murdoch's News International has made the running with Sky Channel, which provides pre-packaged entertainment shows and music videos. There are also two American-owned channels, Screen Sport, run by ABC, and Cable News Network (CNN), run by Ted Turner.

The BBC and ITV are collaborating on Superchannel, which is supposed to provide the best of British programming. Individual companies are also getting involved in ventures of their own. Thames and Anglia are behind a new channel which is to be launched from the Astra satellite, and Granada, ITN and Virgin are the main components in BSB, which is to use Britain's own satellite.

For these companies, satellite is a big gamble. On the one hand they would prefer it not to take off, because it would mean the end to the current system. On the other, they want to be in on it if it succeeds. Certainly they will have to wait a long while before they start to make any profits. There is no guarantee that it will be the success that everybody is predicting. A recent survey by Professor Jeremy Tunstall showed that in Europe the main 'terrestrial' networks still maintained a large percentage of the audience, even where satellite and cable were flourishing. Even in America, the three main networks maintain 70% of the audience. In Britain, the popularity of video recorders may have to an extent satisfied the demand for more choice. But nobody is taking any chances.

The majority of satellite programming will be 'bought in'. It won't be made by the companies themselves. At the moment the profits are not big enough to pay for expensive programme making. It is easier to buy them off the shelf. Therefore much of what is seen, will have already been transmitted on the networks somewhere in the world, and won't differ markedly from much of the present diet of programmes. After all, America makes the vast majority of English-speaking programmes, and BBC and ITV already buy what is reputed to be the best of those. Where satellite can improve on the networks will be in the area of films and sport. If the demand is great enough, it is expected that satellite channels will be able to negotiate the exclusive rights to set-piece sporting occasions.

At the moment, the satellite channels derive their income from selling advertising time, and subscriptions from cable companies. When enough individuals have dishes, it is expected that householders will have to pay a subscription to the channels they wish to receive. They will then receive a special decoding device which will 'unscramble' the signal.

But will the satellite dishes sell? At the moment they are big and bulky, and cost several hundred pounds. There is also a ten pound one-off licence fee imposed by the government. But prices are falling in the same way that video recorders became economical for millions of homes during the 70's and 80's. Quite soon it could be a good investment. Meanwhile the market is slowly increasing, especially where cable is popular. Europe has over seventeen million homes with cable, and Murdoch's Sky Channel, for instance, hopes to reach twelve million of these during 1988.

If the cost of satellite dishes goes down, and they become popular, this could mean that the cable 'revolution' could be by-passed by another one, up in the skies. This in itself could be a disappointment for those who hoped that cable would provide more diversity, and more community programming. Already cable companies are feeling the financial cost, and cutting back, or completely eliminating their local programmes. Where this happens the only new channels available to the consumer are those which come from satellite.

For many there is an irony in satellite programming. For while it expands the number of channels available to any country, it reduces the cultural diversity built up by national programming. Many of the channels are American-owned, and people who choose to tune into satellite are more open to the values and culture of the United States, rather than their own society. Some might argue that this "cultural imperialism" is already present on television due to the high proportion of programmes bought from America. But satellite is not controllable. Nobody can stop programmes being beamed into the homes of British people, short of banning them from having satellite dishes. The Government can try to regulate British satellite channels, but can it stop American or European channels from transmitting a constant diet of sex and violence into the homes of British people?

The question of regulating sex and violence became a big issue for the British Government at the end of 1987. A fire-arms enthusiast went berserk in the English market town of Hungerford, killing a large number of people. The newspapers claimed that he had been motivated by a film he may have seen on television, though little proof of this existed. In any case, the Government decided to announce the creation of a Broadcasting Standards Council, which set a code for British television stations to follow when transmitting programmes which contained sex or violence. This proposal attracted opposition from those who felt it smacked of censorship, and could later be extended to take in the field of news and documentaries. It also exposed a new contradiction between the regulation of our own 'terrestrial stations', and those channels being beamed into our homes from space. How could these be controlled? The Government is hoping that other countries in the Council of Europe will join with them to draw up a Convention which will set standards for programmes transmitted on European satellite stations. But it is uncertain what powers such a Convention would have, and what action it could take on channels which transmitted unsatisfactory programmes. The irony is that the very government which encouraged more 'competition' by encouraging satellite television has realised that it is virtually powerless to stop undesirable programmes being beamed from the skies. Many of the satellite channels already show pornography and violence, which the Government is seeking to control in terrestrial television by establishing a 'Broadcasting Standards Council.'

There are other worries about the growth of satellite. CNN, the news channel run by Ted Turner, is turning into the news agency of the world. It is often easier to buy in your world news coverage from CNN, rather than send your own correspondents at great expense. European channels have already done this, including British stations. The danger is that British people will slowly end up with an American perspective on international events. Yet this is a time when great changes are occurring in the allegiances of European countries to the superpowers, and when the centre of world attention is shifting from Europe to the Far East and Australasia. It is thought that Britain cannot afford to have an American world view when such profound changes are occurring which could affect our allegiances to the United States.

There are other worries about the impact of satellite and cable on the quality of British programming. The new channels will depend for a lot of their income on advertising. That advertising will mean a reduction, in turn, on the commercial network in Britain. They may be forced to move 'down market' in order to maintain the level of audiences and attract back the advertisers. Quiz shows and comedies, with large audience will take the place of documentaries and prestige drama, which attract smaller audiences. The fear is that serious programming will be 'ghetto-ised', and that the quality of British television will suffer as a result.

Such a process has already taken place in isolation on BBC1. In 1986, the new controller of the channel, Michael Grade, took the decision to move its flagship current affairs programme, *Panorama*, out of peak-time to after the news at 9.30pm. This was done with a view to improving its share of the early evening audience. Many people regret that programmes like *Panorama* are no longer in the early evening period, but that is part of the scheduling game when you are competing for audiences. With competition from satellite and cable, such decisions may well become commonplace.

As in newspapers, the innovations promised by new technology in broadcasting could well end up restricting diversity in the media, rather than improving it. Expansion of channels, just for its own sake, does not widen access to the airwaves if they are all run by people who already have substantial stakes in our media. Neither is it likely that companies who are making television just for profit will care about standards or variety of programming. Some of the worst television in the world has been created in countries where there is no regulation, with a free market in programming. The task facing future governments in Britain is how to maintain a balance of regulated, but varied programming, in the face of an expanding satellite service over which they have no control. It is important that television, as the dominant medium, maintains some integrity in the face of developments which could destroy the present system.

CHAPTER THREE

Tricks of the Trade

"Now I know it is a waste of time to talk to the *Sun*, the *Daily Mail*, the *Sunday* and *Daily Express* or the *Telegraph*. If I were to be raised to heaven in a fiery chariot, the *Mail on Sunday* would say I was doing it to avoid the cost of the air fare, and the *Sunday Express* would write that I was running away from Tony Benn."

Roy Hattersley MP
Deputy Leader of the Labour Party

In the last ten years the Press has come under increasing criticism, with many people perceiving it as becoming more trivial, more sensational-ist, more biased and more inaccurate. There are many ways in which readers can be misled by newspapers. Sometimes the intention is merely to get a better story, and sell more newspapers. Sometimes it is because the paper has a political line to sell and feels it necessary to attack its opponents, whether the facts are true or not. We have already shown some examples where facts have been distorted or made up. Here are a few more illustrations of how the reader can be deceived.

Falsification of the Facts

Some striking examples of downright lies have been brought to light by the Media Research Group at Goldsmiths College in London. They have analysed many of the stories used by the newspapers to discredit the left-wing Labour councils in some inner London boroughs. As part of the papers' campaign against the so-called "Loony Left", the researchers found many examples of where the facts just did not match the story.

There was a story that Hackney Council had banned children from reciting the nursery rhyme 'Baa Baa Black Sheep'. It was taken up by the *Daily Star*, the *Sun*, the *Daily Mail*, and other national papers. But in fact the Council did not issue any such ban. The parent-run Beavers' Play Group had sung the usual verses and added a humorous line which ran "and one for the little boy with holes in his socks." Later the same story was spread by the *Daily Mail* about another Labour Council. This time it was claimed that Haringey Council had banned the rhyme at a conference on racism which the borough leaders had been instructed to attend. That too was false. But only one newspaper out of those who ran it, the *Yorkshire Evening Press*, had the decency to retract it, saying that they had run the story from what was now seen to be an inaccurate report.

Then there was what might be called the "Sun-shine story". Camden Council, the *Sun* alleged, had ordered its workers not to call each other "sunshine", and a worker who had called a black colleague by that name had faced dismissal. Wrong again.

Another false story appeared in the *Sun*. It ran a prominently featured report headlined: "Freebie trip for blacks, but white kids must pay. Barmy Brent does it again." The story relied heavily on the testimony of a youth worker called 'Shirley Williams'. In fact there was nobody called Shirley Williams on the payroll of Brent Council. There was a youth worker called Lesley Williams, and he denied ever making any of the statements attributed to Shirley Williams. The researchers from Goldsmiths College showed that there was no colour preference, but no apology was ever forthcoming from either the *Sun* or the *Daily Mail* which later ran the story too.

"Our conclusion was that not one of these stories is accurate", the research report concluded. "A few appear to have been conjured out of thin air. The rest, although loosely connected with some basis of fact, have got important details wrong and are misleading."

Selecting the News

By far the most common distortion, however, is achieved not by telling lies but by the choice of what is to appear. It is possible for editors to highlight stories which provide evidence of the paper's political stance, while playing down or totally omitting items which do not. For example a Conservative paper is more likely to report speeches supporting Mrs Thatcher, or speeches which reveal splits in the opposition to the Government.

When an item of news arrives on the news editor's desk, maybe from a reporter, a correspondent or a news agency like the Press Association, he or she can deal with it in three ways. If it suits the paper, it can put it on the front page. If they don't like the news then it can be put in a couple of paragraphs buried deep in an inside page. If a reader does notice it, they might think it's such a short item, it cannot be very important. And if it really is contradictory to the paper's politics it won't be printed at all. One good example occurred after a vast CND demonstration in Hyde Park in London. It happened on a Sunday, and would normally have expected to be reported in some way on Monday. Nearly all the pro-Conservative newspapers ignored it, even though it had been on the television news bulletins the night before. The *Daily Express* however printed a large picture on its middle pages showing how big the demonstration had been. It was printed with a caption in the first edition. By the time the second edition had been printed, it had been replaced with another story.

Use of language

The use of language is very important in giving readers appropriate images. The Glasgow Media Group highlighted this in relation to television. The same is true in any form of written work, but is particularly significant in news reporting. During the arms talks between America and the Soviet Union, Mr Reagan's statements were often described as "a peace initiative", while Mr Gorbachev is often described as making "a propaganda move." Local councils are very rarely described as "right-wing", but they are often called "extreme". In elections, some papers make a distinction between the seats "that the Tories might win", and those that "Labour may grab". The US backed Contra rebels in the socialist country of Nicaragua are often described as "freedom fighters" or "guerillas". In other countries such rebels are described as "terrorists".

The use of photographs

It is often said that the "camera cannot lie". But it can. One picture may be remembered appearing in the *Sunday Express* a few days before a general election. It showed a Labour leader speaking from a platform in a park with the total audience appearing to consist of ten young children. This was intended to show that Labour meetings were a flop. In fact this had been a very well attended meeting, but the camera had been angled to take the platform and the youngsters while carefully leaving out the audience.

There once appeared in the picture department of a national newspaper a picture of a prize bull with all its attributes proudly displayed. The proprietor's wife, a lady of good breeding herself, was prudish and instructed the picture editor to doctor the photograph, which he did. When the the photograph of the bull appeared without the essential parts, the breeder sent a solicitor's letter alleging that the photograph had damaged his reputation. The editor had to settle with a payment of one thousand pounds.

The use of headlines

The headlines in a paper are not written by the journalist who wrote the story. They are written by the people laying out the pages, the sub-editors. The headlines are very important in giving readers a simple impression of what a story is about, and often it can be a false impression. During the last coal dispute, there was a story in the *Sun* which was headlined "Scargill rocked in back to work rebellion". The story which followed revealed that out of more than 20,000 miners, 90 had voted to go back to work. In the event the strike lasted another eight months.

Self censorship

So what about all these journalists who write for these newspapers?

Aren't they concerned about what is going on? Well, yes to a certain extent. Each year scores of determined people stand up at the annual conference of the National Union of Journalists and attack the injustice of the system that they work for. So why then do they continue to work in it ?

Sociological surveys have shown that the majority of journalists see themselves as being politically left-of-centre. It's not always the view of their colleagues, but it is a fact that many journalists work for newspapers which are politically far to the right of their own opinions. Not everybody is in that position. The truth is that there are not enough decent newspapers for decent journalists. Some are lucky enough to work for one of the few organisations which still practice inquiring journalism. Some are happy to work for right-wing proprietors. A few leave in disgust. But the majority work for organisations which are at political odds with their own beliefs; in other words, they censor their own opinions in order to fit the mould required by the editor.

Self censorship is not the cause of a jaundiced Press; it is one of the symptoms. It does not take long to realise what the newsdesk is looking for and usually a journalist will supply it, even if just for a quiet life. They may justify their work by claiming they would rather change the system from within, rather than from outside the organisation. But the honest ones will admit it is because they are paid well to produce the story, and often they have a mortgage to pay and kids to keep. Once they have written it, it is up to the editor what is done with it.

Journalism is a trade which of course encourages cynicism, and in days of high unemployment, it is not surprising that more people do not complain about the way their work is used. Indeed, they will seek the sort of stories which they know will be used, and ignore those which will not.

It is in the end, up to the individual. There is a choice between becoming unpopular with one's editor, and even a liability, or toeing the line. There are some journalists whose ability gives them independence; others who have strong principles. One journalist who had both qualities was the late James Cameron. Shortly before he died, he gave his views on self censorship:

> "I never paid the slightest attention to anyone's policy, largely because I was unaware of it. For example, the *Express* sent me to India to report on the independence negotiations for which I was enthusiastic. I was wholly unaware that Beaverbrook (the owner of the *Express*), following Churchill, was violently opposed to Indian independence and detested Nehru. I consistently filed copy urging independence and extolling Nehru. I learned later he printed the lot, probably gritting his teeth.
>
> I must, perhaps regretfully, admit to you that I have never been under boss pressure. When the least hint of that arose I quit. My enduring motto was: "This time they may find you out". I never once can remember

thinking: "What do they *want*?" I wrote exactly what I wanted, as well as I could in very trying circumstances, and someone always seemed to want it."

There is no doubt a message there for aspiring journalists. Indeed it is the training of journalists which can be so crucial in fighting self censorship from an early stage in their careers. After training, the only independent guidance comes from the NUJ's Code of Conduct. Its first clause sets the tone for the others by ruling that "a journalist has a duty to maintain the highest professional and ethical standards." The union in fact has a rule (18) which allows journalists to be disciplined for breaches of the code. If this was effective, it might be a useful extra tool for improving the standards in the industry. Self-regulation by individual journalists would be more effective than the 'self regulation' practised by the Press Council on behalf of the newspaper proprietors. The disciplinary rule, however, has never successfully been followed through to its logical conclusion — expulsion from the union. It has proved controversial and only tackled on a few occasions. Journalists from all sides of the political spectrum have criticised it as smacking of censorship.

The strength of the final sanction is also in doubt. Even if a journalist was expelled from the union it is unlikely that it would lead to dismissal from the paper. Few journalists' chapels in the national newspaper industry have effective strength to achieve such a result even if they wanted to. There have been self-imposed closed shops in industry, but their members have reacted badly to the imposition of disciplinary action on any of their members. Without the agreement of the chapel, there is little hope of a successful action under Rule 18. With the power of trade unions at a low ebb in the industry, the chances of significant self-regulation are small.

NUJ Code of Conduct

1. A journalist has a duty to maintain the highest professional and ethical standards.

2. A journalist shall at all times defend the principle of the freedom of the Press and other media in relation to the collection of information and the expression of comment and criticism. He/she shall strive to eliminate distortion, news suppression and censorship.

3. A journalist shall strive to ensure that the information he/she disseminates is fair and accurate, avoid the expression of comment and conjecture as established fact and falsification by distortion, selection or misrepresentation.

4. A journalist shall rectify promptly any harmful inaccuracies; ensure that correction and apologies receive due prominence and afford the right of reply to persons criticised when the issue is of sufficient importance.

5. A journalist shall obtain information, photographs and illustrations only by straightforward means. The use of other means can be justified only by over-riding considerations of the public interest. The journalist is entitled to exercise a personal conscientious objection to the use of such means.

6. Subject to the justification of over-riding considerations of the public interest, a journalist shall do nothing which entails intrusion into private grief and distress.

7. A journalist shall protect confidential sources of information.

8. A journalist shall not accept bribes nor shall he/she allow other inducements to influence the performance of his/her professional duties.

9. A journalist shall not lend himself/herself to the distortion or suppression of truth because of advertising or other considerations.

10. A journalist shall only mention a person's race, colour, creed, illegitimacy, marital status (or lack of it), gender or sexual orientation if this information is strictly relevant. A journalist shall neither originate nor process material which encourages discrimination on any of the above mentioned grounds.

11. A journalist shall not take private advantage of information gained in the course of his/her duties, before the information is public knowledge.

12. A journalist shall not by way of statement, voice or appearance endorse by advertisment any commercial product or service save for the promotion of his/her own work or of the medium by which he/she is employed.

The latest proposal by the NUJ to try to enforce its Code of Conduct is an 'Ethics Council', which will "offer redress to the public for the professional excesses of our members." Its main aim is to try to persuade journalists to follow their Code of Conduct, which many have ignored. It will also investigate, and adjudicate all complaints, estimated to be about 200 cases a year. The Council's power, however, will not extend to fining members who break the Code. That power rests with the union executive. The Council will be able to reprimand members who are guilty of breaches not serious enough for further action.

One of the most important clauses in the Code is to "protect confidential sources of information." In the past, journalists have been jailed for not revealing their sources. One television reporter, Bernard Falk, was sent to prison for not revealing the names of republican sympathisers to whom he had spoken in Ireland.

Another case in 1988 was rather different. A financial journalist on the *Independent*, Jeremy Warner, was ordered to reveal the source of an investigative article he had written on insider trading in the City. Despite the threat of a fine or imprisonment, he refused to do so. The

Court eventually fined him 20,000 pounds, which his newspaper agreed to pay on his behalf.

The industrial right of reply

Another form of internal self-regulation has come from the print unions, who have sought to use their power to get changes in the content of their newspapers. That power has been seriously eroded following the move of Murdoch's newspapers to the new electronic site in Wapping. But previously there had been some successes for the unions in attempts to force proprietors to publish replies on certain issues.

The 'Industrial Right of Reply' has been used on occasions for years, but early in the 80's it became a strategy of the Campaign for Press and Broadcasting Freedom. Created in 1979 by the media unions, this campaign has lobbied for reform in the Press and broadcasting industries. It has provided research on the coverage of such topics as the Falklands War and the 1984 coal dispute, in addition to encouraging the launch of new publications. Its main drive, however, has been in developing the Right of Reply, a legal measure to force the media to admit to its mistakes. This is discussed in detail later, but the 'industrial right of reply' was a move to use the industrial muscle of the print unions to get immediate redress for poor journalism.

The Campaign said it regretted having to use such a sanction, but in the absence of reform, they argued that it remains the most effective means of helping people who have legitimate grievances with the media. It is not censorship, they say, because they are merely establishing the right of reply to an allegation, not to remove the allegation completely. When the editor has refused to print a right of reply, it sometimes led to the unions stopping production of the paper. This not only loses sales and advertising revenue for the company, but also loses pay for the printers who decided to take up the case, usually on someone else's behalf.

This use of union power is not new. In 1926, the General Strike was partly sparked-off by the refusal of the machine assistants at the *Daily Mail* to print an article entitled "King and Country", which became notorious as an attack on the loyalty of trade unionists. After the strike an agreement was signed between the proprietors and unions that no industrial action could be sanctioned which interfered with the editorial content of newsapers. For 44 years nothing more was heard. Then in 1970, the unions at the *London Evening Standard* objected to a cartoon satirising a "typical trade unionist". It was published only after management agreed to print a statement from the chapels expressing their objections to the cartoon. Four years later in the middle of the coal dispute of 1974, the NGA chapels at the *Daily Mail* secured the right of reply for the miners' president, Joe Gormley, in response to what was considered as biased reporting of the strike. Then, in 1977, the printers woke up to the power they had at that time, and there were nearly 40 cases where they forced changes on reluctant editors. The most notable example occurred during the health workers' dispute in 1982, and the coal dispute in 1985. Successful action was also taken against biased coverage in elections, and unfair reporting of the Peace Movement. In the latter case, the *Evening Standard* printed a completely unfounded headline: "CND holds hands with the IRA". The printers requested a right of reply, and the editor allowed an article by the CND General Secretary.

The industrial right of reply was at its most effective during the coal dispute of 1984. Even before the strike began, the printers forced the *Sun* to print a reply by the Miners' President, Arthur Scargill, to an unofficial and mischievous ballot form printed in the paper. The *Sunday Times* also bowed to the printers by allowing Scargill to reply to a half-page article by the Coal Board Chairman, Ian McGregor. At the *Express*, SOGAT members eventually forced the proprietor, Lord Matthews , to agree to publish a reply by Scargill to a misleading centre page spread supposedly containing a fictitious speech by the Miners' President which they said he "cannot make" because it was true. Later printers at the *Sun* refused to make up a caption headline of a photograph of Scargill which suggested that the Miners' President was a fascist. On another occasion, no less than four national newspapers printed a picture of a miner who was supposedly "crossing the picket line". When it was confirmed that he was in fact merely reporting for picket duty, the *Sun* and the *Guardian* were persuaded to publish apologies. On June 27, 1984, there was no *Sun*, *Mirror* or *Financial Times*. It was the Miners' 'Day of Action' and the print unions had asked newspapers to carry a short statement putting the miners' case. Three newspapers refused to publish the statement and the printers stopped work, preventing their publication. The others carried it as an unpaid advertisment and were printed as normal.

However unsatisfactory and arbitrary, the industrial right of reply had become an effective weapon for people seeking redress from newspapers. Since then, however, the print unions have effectively had their power removed, and for the time being at least, it is unlikely that this can be a successful tactic for production workers. This is not true of journalists, however, who suddenly find themselves in a true position of industrial power. In the past, they were often hampered in industrial action by the fact that they could not prevent the paper from being published. It was easy for a handful of loyal staff to scrabble together Press releases and Press Association copy and pass it to the printers who usually continued to work. Now it is somewhat different. Not only do they have to write the stories, they also type them straight onto the computerised production system. For the first time they have real power.

It is unlikely that they will use it. Even though delegates at the annual conference of the 34,000 strong NUJ often call for action on Press Freedom, the only response for industrial action from members comes when pay and conditions are discussed. But if journalists were to shed their conservative traits, they could now be a potent force in continuing the tactic of an industrial right of reply.

It has, however, raised the profile of the question of giving proper redress to readers' grievances. At the *Western Daily* Press, the printers chapel negotiated an internal agreement with the editor to allow them to publish a statement in the paper if the journalists disagreed strongly with the editorial content. Among the nationals, Robert Maxwell has appointed a 'Press Ombudsman' for the *Mirror* titles "to give the public a fair deal".

The idea of an Ombudsman first appeared in America when the *Washington Post* voluntarily appointed a former journalist to judge readers' complaints. Over thirty five American and Canadian newspapers now employ their own people to do the same. The concept of the Ombudsman has been described as just good public relations, and there has been little take-up of the idea in Britain. But sometimes newspapers will respond to people wishing for a right of reply. Hilary Benn, son of former Labour Minister, Tony Benn, wrote to the *Sun* complaining about an article on page 2. To his surprise, the full text appeared two days later, in the same space as the original article, but given considerably more space. Such responses are not typical, and of course at present newspapers are under no obligation to print replies.

Co-operative ownership

One response to criticisms of proprietors is to call for more 'industrial democracy', so that journalists and printers can usefully play a part in determining the direction of a newspaper. In France, *Le Monde* is a paper which is controlled by its workforce and its founder members. In Britain, there are at present no examples of national newspapers following that pattern. Two newspapers, however, are run as Trusts. They are set up officially "to see that a newspaper is run in such a way that it continues to serve the best interests of its readers."

The Scott Trust runs the *Guardian* and *Manchester Evening News*, with seven members holding the shares. The Observer Trust partly owns the *Observer* and its members must approve the appointment or dismissal of any editor. Both have been allowed some sort of participation in the selection of the editor. In 1975, Peter Preston was chosen as the new editor of the *Guardian* by a selection committee of trustees and four journalists. More recently, Donald Trelford, the editor of the *Observer*, received the protection of his Trust when the proprietor 'Tiny' Rowlands tried to sack him from the post. Both men are among the longest serving editors in national newspapers.

But Trusts do not protect a newspaper completely from a determined proprietor. Times Newspapers had four national figures on its board, who were there supposedly to protect the independence of the editors of both newspapers. They proved useless in preventing Murdoch from taking over the paper, as the former editor of the newspaper, Harold Evans, testifies. Times Newspapers now in fact have six independent directors who were appointed in 1981 as one of the conditions that Murdoch's bid would not be referred to the Monopolies and Mergers Commission. Their function is to safeguard editorial integrity at the newspapers. Nothing was done, though, to stop the sudden and unpopular move to their new plant at Wapping.

The *Scottish Daily News*

A more radical departure from the normal form of ownership was the co-operative established to take over the *Scottish Daily Express* plant when the paper moved to Manchester. The redundant workers decided to use their pay-offs to fund a workers' co-operative in Glasgow. The building was bought from the *Express* with money raised by the workers, proceeds of a public subscription, some government funds, and a large personal shareholding from publisher Robert Maxwell (who was making his debut on the newspaper scene).

The organisational structure was radically new to Britain, and revolutionary compared to the autocratic style of management which the workers had just left behind. The structure in practice consisted of the Works Council, which had complete control of management and policy making, and the Investors Council, whose responsibility was to elect two people onto the executive and report to shareholders. The Works Council consisted of five members of top management and seven employees elected from the workforce. A dispute would go from the Union chapel, which had the day-to-day responsibility for running the department, to the Federated Chapel, which represented all the unions. If it could not be resolved at this level it would be referred to the Executive Council, which ran the newspaper.

The actual concept of co-operative ownership and publication only lasted for two months. Then the financial insecurity led to the main shareholder, Robert Maxwell, becoming the Chief Executive, and the experiment was effectively over. Within four months the paper was dead. The question people asked afterwards was, could the paper have survived if it had not been for the co-operative control of management? Certainly many of the workforce were happy to have workers' control if it meant survival. If it did not, they were just as happy to have something else. It was very perplexing for the top business management who had been drafted into the enterprise. The management say they found their hands tied on many decisions because the workers had greater voting power on the Council. As the General Manager, Eric Tough, said:

"I saw a huge educational programme that had to be done before these guys would get away from the emotive idea of workers' control. We might have aspired to that after a year or two, with them learning the nuts and bolts of running a business. But to expect them to make viable commercial decisions straight away was an awful lot to hope for."

Predictably, one of his main commercial worries was that the editorial content was too left-wing to attract advertising. Inevitably, in newspapers, commercial decisions are seldom divorced from those on editorial policy.

The alternative press
Over the years other newspapers have tried to become established using different models of ownership from conventional proprietorial control. Most of these papers have been weekly, and all have struggled to survive financially. Some were born out of the alternative papers of the sixties, but by the seventies, they were concentrating on more conventional issues, like council corruption, housing, environmental pollution and local politics.

Perhaps the most successful, and best known, is the *City Limits* co-operative which was set up by former staff of *Time Out* after a dispute about the direction of the magazine. It has now survived for several years, and though salaries are low, and the accounts are precarious, it has established a healthy circulation in London with a mixture of investigative journalism, listings, music, lifestyle and politics.

The others have mostly been co-operatives based in the community, adopting brash investigative journalism, usually from a left-wing stance. Their basic problem, predictably, is organisation and money. Where they have survived, they often stumble on from crisis to crisis, with little continuity and erratic publication dates. In fact the ones that continued the longest, like *Leeds Other Paper*, *Rochdale Alternative Press*, *Tameside Eye* and *Brighton Voice*, were papers which adopted few of the characteristics of the conventional Press. Their strength lay in well developed links in their area and a healthy disrespect for those who see themselves as leaders of their respective communities.

Two other magazines aimed at a national audience. *Rebecca* was an investigative monthly for Wales, and the *Leveller* was an investigative fortnightly aimed at Britain. They were both run by collectives, based on a small core of semi-professional staff and enthusiastic volunteers. The reason for their demise was a lack of advertising, and hence income, necessary to promote the publication and expand the solid base of loyal readers.

Another strand of newspapers sought to challenge local monopolies on a more professional basis. Their aim was to provide weekly newspapers, with conventional systems of advertising and distribution. The model was the highly successful *West Highland Free Press*, a co-operative newspaper with its own printing press and a healthy circulation in the Highlands and Islands of West Scotland. However, when its founder, journalist and now MP, Brian Wilson, tried to repeat his success in Glasgow with a radical weekly paper called *7 Days*, the project failed. The same fate hit the *Dundee Standard*, *Hull News* (a trades council backed paper), the *Nottingham News* (staffed by journalists sacked from an anti-union employer) and the *East End News* in London. The latter's failure during the early 80's was disappointing because it had based itself on a unique 'readers' co-operative' with more than a thousand members. It also had an initial start-up capital of 19,000 pounds, and more substantial sums were raised during its nine months of publication. The problem, as ever, was advertising. It suffered badly from a cut price advertising war with its local rival which was intent on driving it out of business. It also proved how much backing is needed to overcome such pressure.

A feasibility study for a radical weekly newspaper called the *Birmingham Inquirer*, which was never published, showed that initial capital needed in 1982 was at least 85,000 pounds to stand a chance of producing a competitive weekly newspaper over the first year. The *Manchester Flash*, which did appear about that time, collapsed three months after its launch with over 100,000 pounds in debts. It had been started by two professional journalists with initial capital of over 80,000 pounds. It had a substantial professional staff, new equipment and smart offices. Undoubtedly it could have been run better, but it does illustrate two basic truths. Huge amounts of capital are necessary even to start up a small weekly newspaper. And advertisers are always sceptical and play an important role in the success or failure of any publication.

A final point before we leave these newspapers. Whatever their successes and failures, their standards of journalism or the accuracy of their accounts, the people who worked on all these papers have kept alive a belief in an accountable, diverse and free press at a time when conventional papers were closing and the market was shrinking. Many of the projects they began have failed. But they have done more for the principles of good journalism than all the 'free-sheets' which are now delivered to households and exist solely on advertising. If there had been more support from local councils and trade unions for some of these radical papers, they may well have survived.

The experience of these newspapers, and the failure of the *Scottish Daily News*, should have left some lessons for the next people on the road of launching a paper for the Left. In the event, despite the advantages of new technology, it could be said that they made even bigger mistakes. The story of *News On Sunday* follows next.

CHAPTER FOUR

New opportunities with new technology?

"Eddie Shah, the union breaker, may not strike one as any more attractive a prospect than some of the daily press barons, and his much publicised daily when it appears..may not do much to fill the gap between the tit-and-trash lightweights and the textural heavies, but one may hope it succeeds for one objective reason...it could lead the way back to the plurality that is the nature of journalism."

Journalist Tom Baistow

Since those words were written, Eddie Shah's "much publicised daily" has appeared, struggled and been swallowed up into the empire of one of the "daily press barons", Rupert Murdoch. The example of *Today* unfortunately has shown that new technology on its own does not necessarily "lead the way back to the plurality that is the nature of journalism."

It has always been accepted that the best way to reform newspapers is to provide the conditions in which a free and varied Press can flourish. The introduction of new technology into the newspaper industry in this country encouraged speculation that it could provide the answers to critics of our existing system. The argument went that computerised typesetting and printing provides the technology to set up newspapers with a smaller fund of initial capital. Consequently newspapers of all political persuasions can flourish and direct intervention in the Press is not necessary.

New technology has certainly strengthened the hands of the existing Press. After initial investment in new plants, they will now be able to work with far lower overheads. But for the new newspapers it has not been so easy. The *Independent* has done best, with a rising circulation and a well-respected product. There have been some anxious moments and the paper only began to show a steady profit in 1988, nearly two years after its launch. It has been a considerable achievement, possible only because of new technology. The future should be bright, but it has no large corporation behind it if things start to go wrong. The *Guardian* for instance, at least has the profitable *Manchester Evening News* to buttress it against economic storms.

Eddie Shah's *Today* has not been so lucky. After the initial publicity, things started to go wrong. There were technical problems, and it did not increase its circulation fast enough to overcome its own lack of cash reserves. The paper was criticised for being too lack-lustre and not having strong opinions. Under Eddie Shah it had been a supporter of the Alliance which itself was criticised for being too middle of the road and having no real policies. After the General Election of 1987, *Today* followed the example of the Alliance and broke up, leaving Mr Murdoch to buy the paper and Mr Shah to retreat to his minor publishing chain in Warrington, where he announced that he was thinking of starting another daily newspaper, this time with a less ambitious target circulation.

It is true that the new technology requires lower initial capital, but the difference is like silver and chrome; you still have to have a substantial pot of gold to enter the industry. Look for instance at the investment in new technology by the existing newspapers. Murdoch's News International spent 72 million pounds in order to transfer the printing of the *Times*, the *Sunday Times*, the *Sun* and the *News of the World* to Wapping in East London. The *Daily* and *Sunday Telegraph's* new plant on the Isle of Dogs cost 75 million pounds. The *Guardian's* plant in the same location cost at least 15 million pounds, and the new plant for the *Daily Mail* and *Mail on Sunday* will cost over 100 million pounds.

It cost over 20 million pounds to set up *Today*. It was not easy for Shah to raise the money either. The project which involved 'direct input' and the use of satellites for printing was seen as a risky venture by the City. In the end he raised the money by appealing to those companies and individuals who had admired his anti-union stand at Warrington. Most of them were staunch Conservatives who saw his newspaper as an important weapon in the war against old established union practices. Ironically he also received support from two unexpected sources. The Hungarian National Bank put up the six and half million pounds needed to fund the printing presses, and the Electricians' Union, the EETPU, agreed to a no-strike deal in exchange for a single union agreement. This bypassed the traditional print unions like NGA and SOGAT, and this agreement was copied by Murdoch when he moved to Wapping.

The original plan for *Today* was for it to be printed at five centres around Britain, employing 700 people, of which 130 were journalists. The break-even point for the circulation of *Today* was an average sale of 800,000. The paper also had a Sunday edition which was killed off when things began to go wrong. Shah had hoped that this radical reduction in staff, which was roughly half of that normally employed on such a paper, would provide a stable economic base on which to build his circulation. In the end it did not, but he had won the battle with the unions which the other newspapers had not relished. He had been the foot-soldier who had created the gap which the rest of the Fleet Street cavalry charged through, leaving him battered and bruised. Nearly every national newspaper has now managed to negotiate staff reductions and new technology because of the precedents set at *Today*. The move of Murdoch's papers to Wapping only reinforced their position.

The twenty million pound launch of *Today* is small compared with the launches of most newspapers, and perhaps explains one of the reasons for its eventual collapse under Shah. Associated Newspapers had to endure losses of millions of pounds before the *Mail On Sunday* became profitable. And the rest of Fleet Street has only managed to invest in the new technology because of the windfall caused by the stock market flotation of the international news agency, Reuters. Most newspapers had a share in the agency and benefitted from the flotation.

The interesting thing about both *Today* and the *Independent* is that they are both papers of the middle ground. Their view of concensus politics fitted uncontroversially into an area already well covered by the Press. As journalist Paul Foot says; "The more national newspapers there are, the more difficult it is to tell them apart." The area which is under-represented, however, is on the left of the political spectrum, and when the Left tried to follow Mr Shah's example, it failed.

News on Sunday

Ever since the left-wing *Daily Herald* folded in the early sixties, the labour movement has talked about having another newspaper of its own. There have been motions at conferences, and feasibility studies, but until 1985 nothing really happened. It was then that plans were drawn up for *News On Sunday*, a popular left-wing paper which would only appear once a week, and therefore be cheaper to launch.

Previous to *News On Sunday*, the TUC had funded a two year feasibility study to see if it was possible to establish a daily paper for the labour movement. The study chairman, Lord McCarthy, reported that it would cost £6.7 million at 1983 prices. Some of its critics argued that it would be better spending that money on weekly co-operative papers in every major city in the country. The general concensus however was that Labour needed its own daily newspaper. The TUC General Secretary, Moss Evans, outlined what sort of paper it would be.

"It would be a national daily, a similar size to the *Sun*, the *Daily Mirror* and the *Daily Star*, It might look more like the *Daily Express* or the *Daily Mail* than the other tabloid papers, but the content would be radically different.

The news coverage, particularly coverage of the trade union movement, would be fairer and more accurate. There would be sports coverage, entertainment and crosswords, but sensationalism, gimmicks amd sexual exploitation would be out.

It might not be the sort of paper that would suit everyone. But we would appeal to those who want more balanced news than they get in their present paper, and who are sick of the anti-union, anti-labour line peddled in most of the papers."

McCarthy's market survey results showed that it could well outsell the *Times* and the *Guardian* with such a format. In that case the new paper would comfortably exceed the 300,000 circulation which it was estimated it would need to break even.

That is as far as it got. The proposal was greeted with some scepticism from the people who would have to provide the money, the trade unions. Many felt that the proposed paper was underfunded, and the National Union of Journalists was dismayed to find it would be staffed by fewer journalists than any other national paper in Fleet Street, except perhaps the *Morning Star*. The budget allowed for 40 journalists, less than a quarter of the number of the *Times*, and half of those of the *Sun*. If the paper had wished to take its commitment to investigative journalism seriously, many more journalists would be required. In addition, the cash flow forecasts seemed over optimistic. It showed that revenue would match expenditure within two or three months. That had not happened in the launch of the *Star*, a paper backed by the Trafalgar Group, so it was highly unlikely to occur with a controversial paper run by trade unionists. It was also assumed that advertisers would support the newspaper to the same degree as other popular newspapers. No strong evidence was produced to support this supposition.

It was decided to go to the trade unions to ask for money to raise the £6.7 million. Some of them did pledge money, but two of the biggest — GMBATU and NALGO — did not like the look of the feasibility study, and they said no, effectively killing the project. The experience of *News On Sunday* will no doubt have reinforced their judgement.

Two years of planning culminated on 9th July 1986 with the launching of a share prospectus to raise £6.5 million to start *News On Sunday*. The group which had conceived the idea was not formally linked with either the trade union movement or the Labour Party. They were mostly young enthusiastic volunteers from the Left. They managed to quickly bring together some experienced newspaper people to give the project direction. These included the *Daily Mirror* columnist, John Pilger, and Clive Thornton, the former managing director of the *Daily Mirror*, who had just parted company with Robert Maxwell. As their plans developed, Clive Thornton left the project, and he was replaced by Nicholas Horsley, an experienced businessman who owned Northern Foods, a successful enterprise which employed 25,000 workers. He became the Chief Executive of the Company when it was formed following the share flotation.

It was decided not to make the paper a co-operative, but a private limited company. Safeguards were built in to make sure that it could not be unwillingly taken over by another company. It was intended that its Board of Directors would be drawn up not only to represent the interests of the investors, but also those of the workforce and the founding shareholders who had drawn up the original charter for the paper. Forty per cent of the shares would be held by the investors, who had raised the initial capital. Thirty per cent would be held respectively by the Employee Trust and by the Founders Trust.

In early 1985 a detailed feasibility study was begun with the backing of trade unions, local authorities and the Greater London Enterprise Board. This study was far more professional in its approach than the one commissioned two years earlier by the TUC. Detailed market research was carried out by a reputable company, a dummy issue was printed and a survey of advertising and merchandising was completed. Regional working groups were established throughout the country to discuss what the new paper should be like.

The study concluded that the paper could be a "viable and profitable commercial venture". It was intended that there would be a 50-60 page tabloid newspaper, with a cover price of about 35 pence, and would have to sell about 700,000 to break even. The company contracted Guinness Mahon to organise the share flotation in the city to raise the £7 million which was thought necessary to launch the paper. £6.5 million of this would be accounted for by the share issue; the rest would be raised as a loan.

The share issue was launched in July 1986, and the money had to be raised by 5.00 pm on 12th August otherwise the project would be dead. Initially the take-up was good with large sums being put forward by trade unions, notably the TGWU, and local authorities' pension funds. But there were also disappointments. The Co-operative Society refused to back the project, despite its huge resources. As the closure date drew close there were desperate efforts to raise the shortfall. One of those who came on board at this time was Owen Oyston, a man who had just sold his chain of Estate Agents for £30 million, and who already had stakes in local radio and cable television. His stake gave him a place on the Board, which was to become significant later. In the event, the share flotation just scraped home, and the project was underway.

Almost immediately problems began to emerge at editorial level. The company appointed a former Fleet Street journalist, Keith Sutton, to be the editor. Before long it became clear that there were serious disagreements between him and John Pilger, who had been involved with the project from the beginning. Both had strong views on what the eventual paper would look like, and what it would contain. In the end, the Board backed Sutton, and John Pilger took a back seat from then on. There were also other problems. Somebody managed to lose the application forms of some of those who had applied for journalist jobs. Some very highly experienced journalists were mystified why they had not even received a reply, let alone a rejection slip.

The concept of the paper had been clearly outlined in the share prospectus.

News On Sunday will be an independent newspaper which will be free from ties with political parties, major financial institutions or an individual proprietor. It will have a left of centre editorial policy. *News On Sunday* will be a newspaper with an emphasis on investigative journalism. The newspaper will endeavour to deal with human interest stories in a popular way, but not in the sensationalised and factually incorrect manner often adopted by other Sunday newspapers. It will be an internationalist paper which views events and developments in Britain not only in the local but also the global context.

There was also an Editorial Charter drawn up by the Founders as a set of guiding principles for the paper's editorial policy. It was later said that it helped to frighten off advertisers.

The Editorial Charter supports moves towards decentralisation and towards participatory democracy; supports the civil liberties set out in the National Council for Civil Liberties Charter 1985; opposes increased State power; opposes all forms of sexism and racism; supports workers and trade unions; supports unilateral nuclear disarmament and supports the provision of basic necessities, housing, education and health care, in the form of public services.

There were other differences from the rest of the national Press. There was a stated policy to promote equal opportunity and to make sure that the staff included a significant number of women and black workers, which in other papers was not usually the case. There was also a commitment to give readers a "genuine opportunity of right of reply".

The paper was launched on April 26th 1987, published from Manchester. Almost immediately, things started to go wrong as William Flatau, a journalist on the paper, told us:

"We started with the aim of producing a popular, hard-hitting left-wing tabloid, leaving aside the reams of copy on showbiz, the Royal Family and the soap operas that seem to grace the columns of most tabloids. But things went wrong from the very start. The £1.5 million made available for the advertising campaign was nowhere near enough."

The plans for the campaign had led to an outcry from some of the staff as soon as they saw them. One of the slogans was going to be "No tits, but a lot of balls." This was fine for a paper like the *Sun*, but many people felt it was not appropriate for a paper whose avowed aim was to be non-sexist.

"I don't believe the people at the top had any firm idea of what kind of advertising campaign was wanted", says William Flatau. "When none was produced, they were not prepared to see it through. *News On Sunday* ended the affair by parting company with the agency.

"The estimates of sales were far too high" he says. "The prospectus talked glibly of 800,000 copies a week, but the first issue saw just half a million sales, even though one and a half million had been printed. By the end, the paper was selling just 120,000 a week. The resources of the paper were far too small, and just weeks after the launch we were running out of money. There was no-one on the Board with a firm grip on the accounts with the result that a lot of money was wasted or just disappeared. If nothing was done fast, the paper would close."

Something was done. Although the original constitution had declared that *News On Sunday* would on no account be allowed to fall into the hands of any one individual, it was taken over by Owen Oyston, the man who had jumped on board just before the share issue ran out. Mr Oyston was a man who paid eloquent lip service to the rights of working people, and liked to be described as a socialist who was against the North-South divide, and who believed strongly that the North could once again become prosperous. After some negotiations with the TGWU, who had a substantial stake in the project, a new company was formed called Growfar. Mr Oyston became the Chief Executive and he brought in a new editor.

"After Oyston took control more than half the staff were sacked", says William Flatau. "As more people became disillusioned and left, they were not replaced, and by the end there were just two reporters in the Manchester head office." During this time the remaining workers had to serve under no less than four different editors who succeeded each other with depressing inevitability. "What was really wanted were hard news stories and features about the crumbling NHS, unemployment, low wages, the Stock Exchange rackets and nuclear energy. There were so many issues with good stories waiting to be written about. Instead we were filling the paper with columnists such as MPs and other public figures. That is all very well, but it was not the hard-hitting journalism we wanted to see that seems to be missing from most of the British Press."

On Friday November 20th 1988 at 11.55 am, Owen Oyston announced that *News On Sunday* was to close. According to Brian Whitaker, one of the editors on the paper in the final days, "It was a traditional Fleet Street ending to what began as a radical, mould-breaking project." The paper had lasted seven months. Oyston was left with the paper's debts, but also a city centre office, up to date editorial equipment with computers, and other assets.

As the dust settled, stories began to emerge about how the unique form of management worked in the early days. Brian Whitaker, writing in the *Guardian*, described the run-up to the launch while the new editorial team were producing dummies. "After each dummy the founders would harangue the editor and senior journalists for hours on end at product development committee meetings. It was at one such meeting that a founder told the editor to stop using rounded corners on pictures for the TV page because they were "politically reactionary".

"Meanwhile, the enormous marketing department was entertaining minor showbiz stars to lunch at Groucho's Club in Soho", continues Whitaker. "Almost none of the marketing staff had ever worked in marketing. They were mainly people who had helped with the paper's initial fund-raising. The reason for the Groucho lunches was described as 'below the line marketing', whatever that meant, though I doubt whether they brought the paper a single extra reader."

The remaining question is where does the experience of *News On Sunday* leave the aspirations of the Left of owning and running its own national newspaper? "The whole exercise seemed to show that the Left in Britain are unable to organise themselves", says William Flatau. "The endless committees which saw through the papers first few weeks are not the way to run a newspaper." It is certainly true that the *News On Sunday* debacle has put back the Left's aspirations for many years. Local authority pension funds and trade unions are always going to cite the case of *News On Sunday* when they are approached for money in the future.

Charitably it might be said that at least they tried, and that lessons can be learned. Mind you, that was said after the demise of the *Scottish Daily News*, and many of the same problems persisted. From an outsider's point of view, there seems little substance in the charge that it was the complex organisational structure which was to blame for all the problems. It seems that it was lack of experience, lack of a firm concept of what the paper would be, and lack of money to put it right. The *Independent* got it right first time, and they had to, because they had no resources to fall back on. But there are national newspapers existing today which started life as poorly as *News On Sunday* (*The Mail on Sunday* is one example). What they had was the backing of a substantial company to get things right, and more starting capital in the first place.

It must be said that the whole episode of *News In Sunday* is not all doom and gloom. It proved that a popular newspaper can be published which seeks to follow the highest standards of journalism, without pandering to the lowest common denominator. There is little doubt that its first few editions left something to be desired, but slowly it was beginning to settle down, and become more consistent. Nobody on the Left of British politics could have complained at the colour section on the Sunday before the June General Election. Others would have been impressed with the populist way that serious topics were covered. Indeed, despite the criticisms, *News On Sunday* did a lot of things right. It just ran out of breathing space to consolidate on what it had achieved. It would be a pity if the example of *News On Sunday* was always used to prevent further projects of this kind, because it provides a working model which, when amended, could be used as a starting point for future newspapers of the Left.

The case of *News On Sunday* is even more ironic when you consider that it was the best planned, the best funded and the most professional attempt at starting a left-wing paper seen in Britain for many years. And still it failed. Surely it goes to prove that the existing system, with or without new technology, is not able to put right the inequalities of our national Press industry? New technology on its own is certainly not the panacea which some commentators expected it to be. The wholesale reform of the Press is still very much on the agenda.

CHAPTER FIVE

Paper Chains

The Existing Constraints on the Media

This country differs from many others in that it has no laws which relate specifically to the media. Newspapers, radio and television are constrained only by their adherence to legislation which covers wider areas. To most people this is a desirable aim, but it is also full of flaws. Readers, for instance, are not protected from receiving one-sided information, or being the victims of inaccuracy or sensationalism.

Laws which exist in other countries are designed to protect the public from the worst excesses of journalism. In this country we have settled for self-regulating machinery. Newspapers are supposedly policed by the Press Council, a body financed by the industry and dominated by people who have worked in it. The same is true of the Broadcasting Complaints Commission which adjudicates over complaints in television and radio. If these self-imposed restrictive chains were strong enough to protect people from excessive practices, and yet still preserve the independence of the media, there would be few complaints. But both bodies have had occasions when they have failed in both respects. They have either been unable to stop newspapers from printing lies or discriminatory stories, or else they have failed to take a strong lead in protecting the industry from laws which prevent the media from operating in a free way.

Now the Government is proposing to add a new body to the regulatory process in the guise of the Broadcasting Standards Council. This is supposed to adjudicate on standards and taste, but has already been condemned as a "Council of Censorship".

The public's 'right to know' continues to be eroded by a constant stream of common law and legislation which affects the way that journalists gather information or report it. It is not just the over-restrictive libel laws which have protected generations of corrupt politicians and businessmen. Secrecy laws can either prevent civil servants from disclosing information or prevent journalists from publishing it. 'D' notices are a government device for censoring news. The Prevention of Terrorism Act prevents journalists from interviewing representatives of banned organisations without first telling the security forces. The 1981 Companies Act relaxed the legal obligation on private companies to provide up-to-date information on

63

their business transactions, thus avoiding proper scrutiny by journalists. The Contempt of Court Act can stop journalists from reporting vital evidence or commenting on a case which is going to appeal. The Police and Criminal Evidence Act threatened to allow police to apply for a warrant to search a journalist's premises for unpublished information or papers which could identify the source of information. Only quick lobbying by journalists prevented this clause becoming law. There have been attempts to use 'breach of confidence' as a way of suppressing important disclosures. Commercial companies and the Government have both mounted civil actions to try to prove that such revelations have breached a person's Contract of Employment.

New potential restrictions exist in the Copyright, Designs and Patents Bill which would theoretically give the right of authorship to anyone who gives a television or radio interview, and possibly even a newspaper interview. This would give an interviewee who thinks he or she did not perform well, the right to stop it from being broadcast. This would make it very difficult to proceed with the serious questioning of government ministers and other people in the public eye.

The recent Local Government Bill, through its Clause 28, sought to prevent local authorities from promoting homosexuality. It was never clear how this was to be defined and whether its interpretation would also include local media.

Another bill, on the Right of Privacy, would make it extremely difficult to investigate the backgrounds of politicians and businessmen who are believed to be acting against the public interest. There is no doubt that the harassment of private individuals in order to write sensationalist or titillating stories is undesirable. But it requires a delicate balance to prevent such occurrences, without stopping some of the important roles of journalism such as investigation and exposure which are in the public good.

So existing constraints on the media are weighted heavily against disclosure and do not provide the protection for innocent individuals. More often they are used by the very people that journalists are often seeking to expose. So how do these self-regulating bodies work?

The Press Council
The Press Council was set up in 1953 as an attempt to stave off demands for legislation which were still in the air following the Royal Commission on the Press in 1948. Newspaper proprietors were fervently opposed to its creation but eventually succumbed to parliamentary pressure. Its role is to campaign against the erosion of the 'freedom of the press', to act as a watchdog on the ethics of journalism and to adjudicate on complaints from the public about stories that appear in newspapers. Many people feel that it fails to fulfil

any of these tasks properly.

As we have just seen, it was powerless to prevent the plethora of legislation which has come along over the last twenty years and now restricts journalists from revealing important information. It has been powerless to influence the ethics of an industry and the sort of sensational 'cheque-book' journalism which surrounded the reporting of the trial of Peter Sutcliffe, otherwise known as the Yorkshire Ripper.

The case was a test of the influence of the Press Council. After a two year inquiry, it severely criticised the offering of 'blood money' for the stories of people who knew Peter Sutcliffe. It censured seven newspapers for breaking the Council's own 'Declaration of Principle' on cheque-book journalism. But the Press has ignored the censure and continued its questionable practices. Only a short time later, large sums of money were made available for photographs and stories relating to Andrew Neilson, another man convicted for mass murder in 1983.

Even then it became clear that the industry had been less than frank in giving details to the Press Council over their coverage of the Ripper trial. It was revealed that some newspapers had not declared to their own watchdog body that other payments had been made to friends and relatives of Sutcliffe.

The Sutcliffe case exposed the weakness of the Press Council. It has no power to compel newspapers to do as it tells them, even though it is supposed to act as their 'conscience'. In addition, it has been criticised as being slow to adjudicate on complaints from the public, and powerless to stop newspapers ridiculing their judgements once they are made. Technically newspapers are obliged to carry the results of Press Council adjudications which affect them. But they are usually given less prominence than the original article and can often sting the offending newspaper to repeat the offence by criticising the Press Council's judgement.

This was the fate of several of the 1,444 cases that were submitted to the Press Council in 1986. Out of these only 47 were upheld, and another 10 were upheld in part.

There have been many calls to give the Press Council more teeth to enforce its decisions and impose sanctions against those newspapers who ignore them. But both the Labour Party and the National Union of Journalists have decided that it is too late to reform the Press Council. The Labour Party's manifesto in 1983 said it should be replaced "with a stronger, more representative body". The NUJ withdrew its support in 1980, arguing that participation would only give the Press Council more legitimacy and prolong its life. The TUC first went along with this line, but later reverted to a policy of reform and asked the NUJ to reconsider its own position. The journalists voted to stay out, not because they felt the Press Council was too unreasonable, but because it was ineffectual in maintaining the standards of their trade. So the position stands today. The Press Council retains its present state because it has no internal desire to reform itself. Those outside who disapprove of it have no muscle to conduct the transformation themselves.

Even the Conservative Government bowed to criticism of the Press Council in 1988, and warned newspapers to improve respect for privacy and the system of self-regulation. The warning came in a speech to the International Press Institute by the Home Office Minister, Tim Renton. He said that "Newspapers do not always strike the right balance between liberty and responsibility. Freedoms always carry with them certain obligations. For while it is all very well to harry and criticise a politician for his or her public conduct, it is quite another to intrude mercilessly into the private lives of ordinary men and women, or to pillory those who lack the money to seek redress through the courts."

Mr Renton's speech was unprecedented for a Conservative Minister, as he was handing out a stern rebuke to the Government's friends in the Press. The Conservatives had hidden behind a non-regulatory policy for the Press for many years, but pressure from the Private Members Bills on Right of Reply and Invasion of Privacy had prompted some sort of show of concern from the Government.

The Home Office Minister urged the Press "to realise that, unless it respects the Press Council's findings, the future existence of the council might be called into doubt, and that in such an event it would be inconceivable for Parliament not to replace the council with some other form of regulation. Any system of self-regulation is only as good as the degree of co-operation which it receives from those who are party to the system."

The Broadcasting Complaints Commission
The position with the Broadcasting Complaints Commission is somewhat different. For a start it is a comparatively new body. Set up in 1980 under the Broadcasting Act, it has five members appointed by the Home Secretary for a five year term of office. It replaced two separate bodies which used to hear complaints on behalf of the BBC and IBA.

It has the power to enforce either broadcasting body to transmit a summary of a complaint which has been upheld by the Commission. These adjudications usually appear just after a future programme in the series, and unlike the Press, there has never been a case when a television company has failed to do this in the proper manner. But though the BCC has the reputation of being a watch-dog "with teeth", it is also perceived to have its failings. As Geoffrey Robertson says in his book on the Press Council, the first eighteen months of the BCC "made little impact; eight of its eighteen cases were brought by the National Front, an organisation with the experience and the dedication

yet new
so false.

to overcome its procedural hurdles. It serves to irritate programme makers without contributing to an informed debate about programme standards."

The programme makers find the BCC difficult because they say they already have to answer to the BBC or IBA if they fail to keep to strict guidelines laid down by these bodies. The BCC is an extra tier of control which is time consuming, and which they believe is unwarranted. The record of television and radio is generally accepted to be far better than that of newspapers.

Certainly many of the complainants are large companies which have the means to go to court if they feel they have been misrepresented. The effect of the BCC is to act as a dampener on the sort of inquiring programmes which many people want to see. Companies can also use the Complaints Commission in the same way as a 'gagging writ', in order to dissuade other journalists from following up the story.

A new development in current affairs television sets a new question of fairness. The inception of Channel Four led to a new style of current affairs, which presupposed that so-called 'facts' are in fact the subjective view of the person expressing a view. It was safer to be truthful about this, goes the argument, and present an issue based on partisan discussion, rather than careful analysis by an independent producer. Programmes like *Diverse Reports* on Channel Four, and *Split Screen* on BBC, allow protagonists from either side to present their partisan views and let the viewers make their own mind up who is telling the truth. The idea has many attractions, not least because it takes away from the television producer the chance to play 'God' and adjudicate who is right or wrong. But is such honesty a service to the viewer, who may not know any of the background to the issue before it is presented as two opposing sides. Does it give the viewer a chance to really appreciate the distinction between an authoritative opinion, on one hand, and a spurious fact twisted to support an even more spurious argument, on the other?

Statutory controls

As we have already noted, there is a plethora of laws which prevent journalists from carrying out their jobs properly, from libel laws, through to the Official Secrets Act of 1911. But how successful are the laws which are designed to encourage the freedom of the press? There are not many to choose from; in fact, the only significant measure is the clause against press monopoly, enshrined in the Fair Trading Act of 1973, and revised from initial legislation in 1965. This rules that mergers involving newspapers with a circulation of over half a million should be referred to the Secretary of State for consent. He can choose whether to refer it to the Monopolies and Mergers Commission.

Out of nearly forty submissions that have been made to the Monopolies Commission, only one has been refused, and that was a minor case. It is interesting to note that out of eight major mergers since the legislation was first introduced in 1965, four have been approved by Labour governments. The *Times* went first to Roy Thomson in 1967, the *Sun* went to Rupert Murdoch in 1969, the *Observer* was bought by Atlantic Richfield in 1976, and Express Newspapers was bought by Fleet Holdings in 1977. Both the *Times* and the *Sun* were bought by newspaper proprietors with existing substantial holdings. The *Observer* and the *Express* were bought by large conglomerates with other interests. More recently there have been other acquisitions. The *Observer* was sold by Atlantic Richfield to a British conglomerate, Lonrho, in 1981. This was allowed by the Monopolies and Mergers Commission, but only after certain conditions were imposed on the new proprietor, 'Tiny' Rowland. In 1985 the Express Group was taken over when Fleet Holdings sold out to the United Newspapers Group, run by David Stevens. United's main interests lay in provincial newspapers, and the take-over was approved by the Commission despite objections from the journalists' union. The NUJ had warned the Monopolies Commission that, if it allowed United Newspapers to take over the Express Group, United would be more likely to channel resources into national newspapers and 'rationalise' its regional newspapers through closures. Within the year, United Newspapers closed down the *Sheffield Morning Telegraph*, one of its provincial papers. Also in 1985, the *Daily Telegraph* Group was taken over by the Canadian financier, Conrad Black. No objections were raised by the Commission.

If we look at those seven acquisitions, it might be concluded that, despite their regularity, they have done little to transform the ownership of the national press. But the most worrying aspect does not refer to any of those events. It relates to the continuing growth of Rupert Murdoch's British newspaper empire. Mr Murdoch, not happy with just the *News of the World* and the *Sun*, decided to take over the *Times* and *Sunday Times*. This was allowed to go ahead without referral to the Commission. In 1987, Mr Murdoch acquired the *Today* newspaper. This was also allowed to proceed. Following this, Mr Murdoch began to build up his holdings in the *Financial Times*, owned by Pearson and Sons. The Monopolies and Mergers Commission has conspicuously failed in preventing any of these things from occurring.

One of the considerations for the Secretary of State is whether a newspaper is about to go bankrupt, or is trading in the red. If it is, the merger does not have to be referred to the Commission. In the case of the *Times* and *Sunday Times* in 1981, both the Secretary of State, John Biffen, and the Prime Minister, Margaret Thatcher, concluded that Times Newspapers were making a loss, and thus could permit their sale to Murdoch without referral to the Monopolies Commission. This was despite constant evidence that the *Sunday Times* was in fact making an appreciable profit at the time. In the case of *Today*, there is little doubt that it was in severe financial trouble. But a lot of that was due to lack of back-up resources. At least the Monopolies Commission could have held up the sale long enough to see if there were any other bidders. After all, a shrewd businessman like Murdoch is unlikely to spend £27 million on a paper which he regarded as worthless.

The Monopolies and Mergers Commission has conspicuously failed to prevent the increasing centralisation of the Press. It was hoped that new technology would bring an end to this trend. But with the exception of the *Independent*, this has failed to materialise. *Today* has been sold to Murdoch, *News On Sunday* has folded, and the only newcomer breaking even is *Sunday Sport*, a pornographic tabloid of no journalistic substance. It is so divorced from journalism that it does not really qualify as a newspaper.

In broadcasting, the regulatory authorities have powers to deal with encroaching monopolies. Newspaper groups do have holdings in local radio stations, and some commercial television companies. But there are specific rules governing share ownership in commercial companies. No one group can own a significant proportion of more than one television station. If it wants to buy shares in another franchise operation, it must sell its shares in the existing one. The IBA is also wary of take-overs. It does not believe in awarding a franchise to one group, which is then taken-over by another company. Franchises are not to be bought and sold in the market place, they say. They prefer a share arrangement which provides only a small number of voting shares, held by persons approved at the time of the franchise award. In 1982, the Midlands company, ATV, was bought by an Australian, Holmes a' Court, thus taking control not only out of the country, but out of the Northern hemisphere. The IBA took legal action to bring it back under British control. The franchise was only re-awarded to the new group on condition that their London studios were closed, to be replaced by new studios in Nottingham supplying the expanding East Midlands.

Few people are prepared to argue that the franchise system is perfect, but it has had sufficient success not to be tampered with by successive governments. Now Mrs Thatcher's Government wants to change the system. Whether it will work in favour of maintaining present standards remains to be seen.

CHAPTER SIX

Media Policy over Forty Years

Nobody could say that governments have neglected to consider the media. It is one of the most studied industries in our country. In <u>forty years</u> there have been no less than <u>three Royal Commissions on the Press, and four Committees on Broadcasting</u>. The diligence of these bodies has produced copious volumes of well-intentioned debate about the future of the media. Whether anything has actually been achieved is another question.

The Press
The proposal for the first Royal Commission on the Press came originally from the Manchester Branch of the National Union of Journalists. As a major printing centre and home for the Manchester Guardian, the city had gained a reputation for strong, radical journalism. Just after the Second World War, such radicalism was accepted. The new reformist Labour Government set up the Royal Commission in 1947, which reported back in 1949. Much of the evidence to the Commission centred around how to save the existing papers which were very much in decline. That problem was so great that little attention was paid to balancing the political bias of the Press. Though the Labour Party had been returned to Government in 1945 with the biggest majority in its history, the newspapers were strongly hostile to its policies.

Hannen Swaffer, one of the contributors to the Commission, noted:

> "A new idealism has spread in all classes, except among the selfish few. But today the public is being persuaded in the Press that we are a race of helots. In nearly every city and town in the country, Labour voters whose party has no local newspaper of its own are forced to buy an anti-Labour newspaper in order to read any news of district happenings. So, by their pennies, they build up the power of the newspaper machine which all the time remains their political enemy. That assuredly is a mockery of democracy."

But the frustrations of Labour supporters held no sway with the Commission. It reported that "the decrease in the number of newspapers, which is an aspect of concentration of ownership, has not been so great as to prejudice the public interest." The 1945 Labour Government was not inclined to further antagonise the Press proprietors, and the only significant outcome of the Commission was the setting up of the Press Council.

The 1947 Commission did leave a cautionary note, however. It warned that any "further increase in the number of national newspapers would be a matter for anxiety, and a decrease in the provincial morning newspapers would be a serious loss."

By 1961, when the second Royal Commission was set up, it had to note that "since 1949, seventeen daily and Sunday newspapers have ceased publication in London and the provinces, and the ownership of those which remain has become concentrated in fewer hands."

The failure to act after 1947 had been followed by serious losses, notably the death of the *News Chronicle*, and its London evening paper, the *Star*. The Labour paper, the *Daily Herald*, and its sister, the *People*, were acquired by *Daily Mirror* Newspapers. There had also been dramatic losses in the provincial dailies and evening papers. The variety of the Press was becoming more and more restricted.

The second Royal Commission commended that "it is easier to diagnose the disease, than to provide a cure." It listed a number of recommendations, but once again, only one major change was made as a result of the Commission. This was the introduction of the anti-monopoly legislation in 1965. But, as we showed in the last chapter, this is riddled with loop-holes and has not stopped the concentration of the Press into fewer hands.

After the 1961-62 Commission, newspapers continued to fold. The *Daily Herald* became the *Sun*, later taken over by Rupert Murdoch. In 1977, a third Royal Commission was established in a climate of mounting panic about the profitability of a number of newspapers. Survival, rather than press freedom, was once again the dominant theme. New technology came onto the agenda for the first time, with wide-eyed newspaper executives returning from the United States with wondrous tales of the new dawn of Press production. Journalists were typing their stories straight onto computers, which subsequently set and printed the newspapers. The workforce was substantially reduced and papers were once again profitable.

Yet the Commission knew that the technology had only taken off in America after newspaper proprietors had closed existing plants, sacked the printers, and opened up two days later in modern computerised offices. Less than ten years later, history repeated itself in Britain, with Murdoch's sacking of up to 5,000 printers, and the transfer of the printing to his fortified plant in Wapping, East London. In retrospect, it is easy to say that the Royal Commission should have seen this coming and tried to impose a sensible timetable for conversion to new technology. Management, faced with long-standing restrictive practices of their own making, were reluctant to initiate their own timetable. The print unions in Fleet Street, in their own way, should have appreciated the inevitability and increasing pace of new technology, but given their former intransigence, were unlikely to do so. A firm timetable for new technology from the Royal Commission would have been far-sighted and invaluable today. As it is, out of 73 recommendations from the Commission, nothing significant was ever carried out.

Many of the proposals were actually quite radical, which was surprising given that the Commission's main purpose was to solve the dire economic instability of most newspapers at the time. It recommended, for instance, that journalists should be involved in the appointment of their editors. Only the *Guardian* and *Observer* practise a limited sort of consultation in this way. They recommended that there should be better and broader coverage of trade union affairs, given the noted lack of constructive reporting from newspapers hostile to the Labour movement. They suggested two improvements for the Press Council. First, that newspapers should be forced to publish adjudications on the front page of the paper in question, and secondly, the Council should adopt more stringent standards against the invasion of privacy by newspapers and their reporters. None of these recommendations were implemented.

Moreover, the third and most recent Royal Commission differed from its predecessors by prompting a 'minority' view by two of its members who were shocked by what they called the "complacency" of the report on certain issues. The trade union leader, David Basnett, and Geoffrey Goodman of the *Daily Mirror* wrote "We do not believe it deals with sufficient strength and urgency with the danger facing the British Press. In terms both of economic and democratic development of the Press, there are dangers now which will, in our view, be infinitely more so by the early 1980's." Their main concern was that little attempt was made by the Commission to actually find ways of expanding the number of newspaper titles on sale. Survival was the theme of the report, yet expansion, they argued, was the only way of creating a newspaper industry with a spread of views not dominated by one scenario of the political economy. To do this, some form of government assistance would be needed to assist new titles to come into production.

Basnett and Goodman argued that the majority report was wrong to reject all the proposals for government assistance which had been put to them. Yet they pointed out that in thirteen countries surveyed by Political and Economic Planning, a group which gave evidence to the Commission, some form of government assistance was provided to help sustain a diverse and democratic Press. In not one of these countries had there been complaints that the government had interfered in the Press more than they had previously.

The two dissenters urged the establishment of a 'launch fund', whereby the critical finance would have to be obtained at the normal rate of interest from the market. Alternatively, it was felt that new publications might benefit from the formation of a 'National Printing Corporation' to provide facilities at an intitially favourable rate. Any assistance by State loans or subsidies would come into operation only when circulation and advertising had reached a certain level, say, fifty thousand. This would cease when the circulation had 'taken off' and reached a higher level, say, one hundred thousand.

The minority report was considered by the Labour Government under James Callaghan, but it was obviously felt that the Government's parliamentary majority was too slender to tackle such radical reform. The merits of these proposals are discussed later, but their existence does reflect the main problem of all three Royal Commissions on the Press. They were all constituted to try to maintain the *status quo*, being the same number of existing titles. As such, they all failed because the concentration of ownership has continued despite the recommendations of all three Commissions. None of them satisfactorily addressed the question of the expansion of the Press, either by a growth in the number of titles, or by ownership of the media as a whole. New technology was never perceived by the Royal Commissions as an incentive to expansion, which clearly it is. By ignoring the ideas of the minority report in the third Commission, the expansion we are witnessing today may put new papers on the streets, but how many of them will be set up by groups outside the existing media?

Broadcasting
In contrast to the three Royal Commissions on the Press, the Broadcasting Committees were outrageously decisive. They were established in 1949, 1960 and 1974, and each committee led to a separate Broadcasting Act. The Peacock Committee of 1986 is no different, with a Broadcasting Act expected in 1988. To be fair, the Broadcasting Committees were considering an industry which was rapidly changing, and because of the finite number of broadcasting channels, regulation of some sort was needed.

Also in contrast to the Royal Commissions on the Press, the Broadcasting Committees' main concern was not survival, but a controlled expansion of the medium.This is not to say that there were not criticisms of the structure of broadcasting. The Pilkington Committee, which sat between 1960-62, was heavily critical of the services run by the then Independent Television Authority. It recommended that advertising time should be sold on a central basis, and that the Independent Television Association should buy programmes off the contractors. This recommendation was not taken up. But the Committees did eventually lead to Acts of Parliament.

The first Act in 1955 established ITV, the second in 1966 established BBC 2, and the third in 1982, led to the creation of Channel Four. In addition, commercial radio was launched in 1973, accompanied by a corresponding network of BBC local radio stations. Since 1979, there has been further expansion: breakfast television, daytime television, night-time television, cable television, and now satellite television. Because of the widening spread of output, the Broadcasting Committees have found it easier to answer criticisms of lack of variety, or lack of access to television and radio. The structure of Channel Four was devised to enhance the amount of access of different groups to the airwaves. The proposals on commercial radio are expected to encourage the formation of community stations.

The need is to make sure that these objectives are achieved. There is no point in establishing Channel Four, community cable television, or community radio stations, if in the end they are the same as those which already exist. Many people fear that if television depends upon ordinary commercial market forces to survive, it will actually lose its diversity and its quality. The task for future governments is to make sure as far as possible that the expansion of British television and radio does not lower the standards which have given it its worldwide reputation.

CHAPTER SEVEN

Media Reforms Abroad

One argument constantly used against Press legislation is that any government intervention is a direct threat to the freedom of the media. This principle has been strongly upheld by the three Royal Commissions on the Press. Their reluctance to use direct government intervention on the Press left them with two main proposals after thirty years: the Press Council and the Monopolies and Mergers legislation. Both measures fall far short of direct legislation in the media, and have been shown to have failed. Yet other European countries have not been shy in bringing in laws which directly affect the way their newspapers are run. Indeed, some have passed Press Acts, bringing a degree of regulation to their media industries.

It is inevitable that the success of these measures is open to debate in the countries involved. But the most important factor is that these countries have decided to make some sort of direct intervention in their media. No one has managed to prove that the freedom of the press has been undermined by these measures, though there are many who argue that they have created a better climate in which a varied and free press can thrive. It is possible that some of the experience in other European countries could be applicable in Britain.

The Right of Reply

Perhaps the most significant feature, which is common to many countries, is a legal 'right of reply'. These simple statutes give individuals and organisations a degree of protection against distortion, misrepresentation and misreporting. It already exists in France, West Germany, Finland, Greece, Switzerland, Belgium, Norway, Austria, Sweden, Denmark, and Canada, while other countries such as Spain are considering it.

In France, the right of reply for both private citizens and representatives of organisations has been enshrined in law since 1881. Editors are required under Article 13 of the Press Freedom Act to,

> "insert, within three days of receipt, the replies of any persons, names, of those referred to in a daily newspaper or periodical, on pain of a fine. The reply must be inserted in the same place and type as the article to which it refers, and with no alteration."

During election time the three day limit laid down for insertion is reduced in the case of newspapers to twenty four hours.

Since 1975 in France, the law has been extended to broadcasts on public radio and television, though this only applies to individuals and not representatives of organisations. During the three years up to 1979, the right of reply was only accorded to nineteen people on television and ten on radio. It might be thought that it is pointless to introduce a law which only applied to 29 cases, but its supporters argue that its very existence probably prevented hundreds of offences of this kind being committed on the air.

In West Germany, the right of reply is central to the state Press laws. Any person affected by a factual statement in a printed work can send the editor a signed statement of reply within three months. The reply must appear in the same section and typeface as the original offending text, and will be printed as a letter to the editor. The largest selling newspaper in West Germany is *Bild*, which has a circulation of about 5 million copies a day. It is owned by the controversial Press proprietor, Axel Springer, and its editorial policy is seen as being right wing. Despite this, the newspaper estimated that only fifty counter-statements are published in *Bild* each year.

The magazines, *Der Spiegel* and *Stern* are also very popular. They report that they draw about eighty demands for publication of a counter-statement each, but only about fifteen of them appear as such. About twenty may be changed by mutual agreement and appear in the letters page. The 45 others do not appear at all, either because the individual or organisation does not bother to pursue it after the publisher refuses to comply, or because they lose the injunction procedure after taking the case to court.

In six of the West German states, the right of reply has been adapted to radio; the reply has to be broadcast to the same reception area and at an equivalent time. As in the case of the Press, the broadcasters are not swamped with demands for air-time. NDR, for instance, is one of the big German public radio and TV stations which serves three federal states in the north of the country. It occasionally handles the TV news service for all of West Germany. Its legal department estimates that it receives about twenty demands for a reply each year, of which between 5 and 10 are actually broadcast. The small number of complaints should not be taken as a sign that the law is not working. On the contrary, it could indicate that a legal right of reply has had some effect in improving the standards of journalism in West Germany.

Whatever the reason for the small number of complaints in both France and West Germany, the figures should allay the fears of newspaper proprietors in Britain who fear a flood of complaints if such a measure was introduced in this country. Yet the right of reply has been introduced as a Private Members Bill no less than five times in the

House of Commons and every time it has been unsuccessful. The issue is discussed in full in the next chapter.

Meanwhile, what other measures have been taken in other countries to improve the diversity of their media? An analysis of media controls in other countries shows that an increasing number have adopted strong anti-monopoly measures, and have not been afraid to insist that proprietors should be 'disinvested' of some of their titles, where it is considered that they own too large a market share of the media.

West Germany

The Federal Republic became the first European country to do something positive about the concentration of ownership in its Press. In 1968, a government Commission laid down limits which prevented any one group from controlling too substantial a share of total Press circulation. In the case of newspapers, this was set at 40% of total sales. The company of Axel Springer, which at the time produced 39% of total circulation, was prevented from widening its newspaper assets further. But more crucially, it was forced to sell five of its magazines to reduce its share in that sector below the new circulation levels. For the first time it meant that a government had not only prevented further concentration of the Press, but actually started to dismantle some of the empires already existing. Later this was augmented by further anti-monopoly legislation which refers mergers of over a certain size to a 'Cartel' office for approval. Apart from these measures, newspapers in West Germany operate under the same lines as in Britain. Under the right of property enshrined in the country's constitution, newspaper proprietors are free to set down the editorial policy in the publications they control. There is only one truly national paper, *Bild*, but two others have significant circulations in certain parts of the country. The majority of the Press is regional and owned privately. The Social Democratic Party (the main left of centre party) owns some local papers, but the largest only has a circulation of about 200,000.

Concern about Press Freedom in West Germany has led the major journalists' union to campaign for some say in the appointment of editors-in-chief. At *Stern*, for instance, a magazine with a circulation of nearly two million, an editorial statute now exists which allows journalists the power of veto over newly appointed editors.

The Netherlands

The Netherlands has also taken some interesting measures to maintain the diversity of a Press which has become more concentrated over the last ten years. To do so, they have discussed a scheme of assistance for newspapers which could have far-reaching consequences for industrial democracy in the Press.

Ever since 1967, when advertising began on television and radio, the government has allowed some form of redistribution of advertising back to newspapers. It has been estimated that in its first nine years, television and radio diverted over a million pounds of advertising from newspapers. Initially, assistance was given as straightforward compensation from a fund financed by advertising in radio and television. Later, a permanent fund was established to assist newspapers which had no other means of finance and which were in danger of closure. Grants were available from a five per cent surcharge on radio and television advertising on condition that the newspaper recovered financially within three years, and its progress was monitored by the government.

It was then that moves were begun to continue such assistance and use it to encourage diversity in the Press. The proposal was to provide assistance, which included newsprint allowances and advertising compensation, in return for a binding editorial statute on the paper. The object of the statute was to put on record the newspaper's editorial and political position in a way that could not be usurped by its sale at a later date. The statute would declare its editorial policy as separate from the commercial side of the paper, and give editorial staff the right to be consulted about any possible sale or merger. Such a statute would, of course, be voluntary and only binding if the newspapers sought assistance from the fund. Its importance lies in its acceptance of the desirability of both advertising re-distribution, and of journalists' participation in the editorial policy of the paper. Both these things have been considered in Britain, but never developed.

Sweden

This is another country which has introduced a system of financial support for newspapers in order to maintain a diverse Press. In this case this has been developed along straight political lines. The Swedes had seen over a hundred newspaper titles disappear in just twenty five years, and by 1966, the government had decided to do something about preventing a further concentration of its Press.

Even though there are national papers in Sweden, there is also a very influential regional Press. The aim of the legislation was to give financial support to guarantee the survival of the smaller newspaper in each circulation area. In this way it was hoped to halt the drift of advertising revenue and sales from the smaller newspaper to its more influential competitor. In essence this has meant actually funding the political parties which own or influence the newspapers. As the majority of the Press supported the Conservative Party, the bulk of the subsidy has gone to the 'A-Pressens', the newspapers owned jointly by the Social Democratic Party and the trade union confederation. The financial support has succeeded in maintaining a competitive Press at a time when it was quickly going the same way as regional papers in Britain. By the early seventies the number of communities in Sweden with two or more papers had reduced from 50 to just 20. Since then, however, the slide has stopped, and 19 of those communities have a choice of papers of different political persuasions.

At the inception of the subsidy scheme, there was opposition to what appeared to be selective support for the Social Democratic Party, particularly as it was its government which introduced the legislation. But the 'A-Press' still only makes up twenty per cent of the ownership of newspapers in Sweden, and the newspapers which support both the Conservative and the Centre-Liberal Parties have also received subsidy. Indeed, the largest Conservative newspaper in Sweden, *Svenska Dagbladet* from Stockholm, received about three and a half million pounds in 1984. They have obviously overcome their initial belief that the subsidy was an attack upon the freedom of the press.

The subsidy only goes to those newspapers which have less than fifty per cent of the circulation in a given area. And it has not necessarily saved badly produced papers from closure. The Social Democrats' morning paper in Stockholm went bankrupt in 1984 when the trade unions refused to give it more money. A recent political analysis of the subsidy scheme by an academic suggests it has upheld the right of the non-conservative parties to be heard.

"For one thing it gives the labour movement a voice (or rather 21 voices) in public debate. This moves the perception of 'public opinion' and the 'concensus' several notches to the left. It also gives each issue in public debate a firm anchor on the left so that the floating voters do not just drift into a right-wing view because that is the only one being expressed."

At the same time the Swedes have preserved the proprietorial function of setting the political and editorial content of their newspapers. The Democracy at Work Act specifically excludes newspapers from some of its provisions. Though it allows the workforce a statutory say in some management decisions, it prevents them from having influence over ideological or political decisions in newspapers.

The other major difference in Sweden is the Freedom of the Press Act which gives every citizen the right of access to all public documents. Access can only be refused if the document is covered by the Secrecy Act which covers such confidential issues as national security or personal integrity. Under the Act there is a right to publish without hindrance, even if the subsequent story leads to court proceedings. Sweden is not the only country to have a Freedom of Information Act. The United States and Australia also have them, and journalists in all three countries are more free to cover the sort of stories which could embarrass their governments. The ultimate example, of course, is the Watergate Scandal which was uncovered by the *Washington Post* and led to the fall of the United States' President, Richard Nixon. It has often been said that such a revelation could never have been made in Britain because of the legislation which restricts the activities of journalists.

France

The French have also taken legislative action to preserve the diversity of the Press. The Mitterand government introduced one of its most controversial bills "to limit concentration of ownership and guarantee pluralism in the Press." It was seen as an attempt to control the Press empire of M.Robert Hessant, who owns *Le Figaro* and *France-Soir*, as well as a string of influential provincial papers. The future of the legislation was put in doubt when the Socialists lost power.

There is however an initiative in France which plays an important part in preserving some integrity in the country's publishing output. This is its unique system of guaranteeing the right of publishers to have their newspapers and magazines distributed and displayed in newsagents. In Britain, wholesalers can refuse to handle publications they do not like. W.H. Smith, for instance, did not stock the satirical magazine, *Private Eye*, for many years, despite its large circulation. In France, the law says that the publishers themselves should run the distribution network, and consequently it is possible to buy a wide spread of publications of all political colours.

The system is best described in a pamphlet from the Minority Press Group. The system was set up in 1947 following a feud between Hachette, the major distributor before the Second World War, and its new rival which objected to the other company's involvement with the German occupation forces. The competition between the two rivals threatened the welfare of the Press to such an extent that a law was passed which ruled that distribution should not be run by competing commercial companies, but by co-operatives which represented the publishers. At the same time it made it compulsory for newsagents to display any publication supplied to them. The essential principle was that there should be "unrestricted distribution of the printed word".

Distribution in France is now run by a private company called NMPP. Fifty one per cent of its shares are in the hands of the publishers, and the other forty-nine per cent are owned by Hachette who continue to supply the equipment and organisation to do the job. The publishers themselves are grouped in five co-operatives, one for daily newspapers, the other four for magazines.

The law has not led to a rush of unreadable, poorly printed magazines lying unsold in piles in newsagents. The publisher, after all, has to pay the initial printing cost, as well as paying for the return of the publication if it is unsold. So there is no point in flooding every newsagent in France with your magazine if you know that nobody is going to buy it. But at least it means you can find out if there is a market for a new publication, and by computer analysis, target it at the areas where it proves most popular. Certainly it has meant that the traditional Parisian street vendor has a far more colourful display than a London counterpart. Neither are there any shortages of people wanting to take on newspaper kiosks as a business.

Apart from its unique distribution system, France also has one of the world's best examples of a newspaper controlled by the people who write for it. *Le Monde*, based in Paris, was founded in 1944 by its first editor, Hubert Beuve-Mery, with support from General De Gaulle. It is a private company which is controlled largely by those who work in it. Forty per cent of the shares are owned by journalists, five per cent by blue collar workers, five per cent by white collar workers and ten per cent by the editor in chief on behalf of the management. The remaining forty per cent are owned by fifteen individuals, most of whom had a part to play in founding or developing the paper.

Important changes in the paper, such as the appointment of a new editor, have to be first approved by the journalists and then it has to go to a full meeting of the shareholders. The newspaper has gained a reputation as being an objective paper which provides a diary of record as a public service. It enjoys the sort of prestige which was once accorded to the *Times* in London. Its editor for 25 years, Hubert Beuve-Mery, admits there is no clear-cut solution to the problem of who decides editorial policy. "An alliance between journalists and the readership is preferable", he says.

Le Monde has not found the economic going very easy. During the early eighties circulation and advertising revenue slumped, leaving the paper nearly seven million pounds in debt. Much of the French Press also suffered, with increased competition from radio and television. At one point it was thought that *Le Monde* would close completely, but the election of a new editor-in-chief has re-invigorated the newspaper and its future looks secure. Critics argue that some of the paper's problems stemmed from the election of the previous editor, and the crisis would not have occurred if the appointment had been left in the hands of commercial management, rather than damaging infighting within the journalists' ranks. In reply it is said that the appointment of an editor is always a tortuous decision. They say that there is no evidence to suggest that the appointments at *Le Monde* have been any worse than some made in Britain over the years. The important thing, they argue, is that the paper's integrity survives.

America

Apart from having a Freedom of Information law, America also has control over the ownership of the media. The Federal Communications Commission has power to regulate any excessive concentration of the media. The United States has few genuine national newspapers, so the emphasis is on preventing monopoly of media ownership in individual States and cities. Murdoch was recently prevented from owning a newspaper and a television station in the same city. He owns newspapers in two of America's politically most important cities — the *Boston Herald* and the *New York Post*. He also has plans to set up a fourth television network, and he became an American citizen to help him realise his dream. Murdoch had been hoping that the media regulations would be waived in his case, but a group of Senators blocked it in Congress, and now he may be forced to sell one, or both, of the papers. It is expected this will lead to a lengthy court battle which will have repercussions on the very nature of the media laws.

Meanwhile in **Australia**, Murdoch owns nearly 70 per cent of the total newspaper circulation. New laws introduced in 1988, however, are designed to prevent proprietors from having interests in other media. As the Minister for Transport and Communications said, "Proprietors will have the choice of being queens of the screen, princes of print or rajahs of radio." The law prevents anyone with more than a 20 per cent share in newspapers from having wide interests in television and radio as well. For instance, under the law proprietors will be barred from controlling a radio station and more than 15 per cent of a newspaper or television station serving the same market.

Similar laws apply in **Italy**. Italian Press proprietors are now forbidden to own more than 20 per cent of the sales in any market.

Overall, the overseas trend is to take the media seriously as an essential part of a country's constitution. In Britain, we have no formal constitution, which may explain why successive governments have been unable to find grounds for a policy of reform in the media. This is not to say that proposals have not been put forward. As we shall see, some of the current ideas come from the systems that other countries use to regulate their media.

CHAPTER EIGHT

The People and the Media

"Over most of this century the labour movement has had less newspaper support than its right-wing opponents. Its beliefs and activities have been unfavourably reported by a majority of the Press."

Royal Commission on the Press, 1977.

The Labour Party has always had a difficult relationship with the Press, so it is not surprising that the majority of the proposals for reform have come from the left of the political spectrum. Both in government and outside, the Labour Party has constantly debated the issue, but actually done very little to change the system which has existed for over a century.

The one question many people ask is: if the Press is so biased, why has Labour been elected to government at all? The answer is not simple. When both Conservatives and Labour were balanced equally, a protest vote against the sitting government has often been enough to secure victory for the other side. After 1945, there were years of consensus politics with little to choose between the two major parties. In 1983, however, a genuine radical choice opened up between them. Mrs. Thatcher offered a truly right-wing government, and Michael Foot's Labour Party went to the country on several radical policies, including a controversial commitment to unilateral disarmament.

It was in this election, far more than the previous ones, where the Press played a significant role. The issue of nuclear disarmament was one that could be put over very simply in tabloid terms. Either one opts for 'strong government', or we 'leave Britain defenceless'. Now that was not the choice being offered, of course, but it played simply into the hands of the headline writers and into people's minds. There is no doubt that the Labour Party could be accused of being naive to expect a hostile Press to present a fair summary of such a controversial policy. But it was a classic illustration of how newspapers can influence elections. Labour canvassers were hearing that morning's headlines being regurgitated to them on the doorsteps the same evening. People may have brought the paper that morning for the sport or television pages, but the subliminal impact of the headlines on the front page inevitably have an influence on people's opinions.

In 1987, Labour once again tried to do the same thing. This time, though it was better presented, nuclear disarmament was still a dominant factor in the newspapers' campaign against Labour. Some people in the Labour Party are now beginning to argue that while the Press stays as it is, it will never be possible to argue any radical policy which can so easily be misrepresented by hostile journalists.

Yet in the four years between the elections, the talk of media reform took a back seat in the Labour Party. In the past it had been seen as an important pre-requisite to fulfilling its ambitions. The Labour Party since 1945 had had standing committees on the media and many of them came up with new proposals for shifting the political bias of the majority of the Press.

Labour's proposals up to 1983

In 1974, fresh from an election victory, the Labour Party published a discussion paper called 'The People and the Media'. It was the result of two years' work by a policy committee led by Tony Benn MP, and few people would quarrel with its intentions.

> "Our aim must be to devise a framework for the media that avoids the twin charges of government or commercial control."

The publication of 'The People and the Media' coincided with the announcement of the appointment of the Annan Committee on Broadcasting, and a Royal Commission on the Press. It was made clear by the Labour Party in their submission that they "absolutely reject any policy for the mass media, or any system for operating, that is based upon government censorship or central control."

Their first commitment was to a more open society, and the proposal was to relax existing restrictions on the freedom to publish, and to obtain information.

> "We think that the Official Secrets Act should be replaced by a Freedom of Information Act which provides statutory protection to individuals and to newspapers and broadcasters seeking official sources of information, putting the onus on the public authority to justify withholding public information."

Three years later the Labour Government showed their concern for protecting journalists by prosecuting two of them under the same Official Secrets Act. Instead of abolishing it, they used it to increase the level of secrecy in government, and thus further restrict the media. In the same way, it was generally acknowledged that the Labour Prime Minister, Harold Wilson, had consistently attacked the media in opposition, but proved a master at manipulating it while in office.

The Conservative Government, of course, has gone on to use the Official Secrets Act in a far more profound way by prosecuting two civil servants, Sarah Tisdall and Clive Ponting, for leaking information to the Press. Neither leak was a threat to national security, but both reflected genuine areas of public concern over government thinking. Similar prosecutions have not been taken against senior members of the armed forces who have consistently leaked defence information to the media as a way of mounting a lobby against cuts in their departmental spending. The government was exposed for doing its own leaking during the so-called 'Westland Crisis' of 1986. The Prime Minister's office was said to have approved the leak of a letter during the ministerial row over who was to take over the Westland Helicopter company. Two Cabinet members resigned during the controversy, but no action was ever taken against the person who leaked the letter.

In 1987, police used the Offical Secrets Act to raid BBC Scotland and to seize the files of journalist Duncan Campbell who was preparing a programme on the Zircon satellite. The programme contained interviews with former senior civil servants, but it was banned.

Later that year, newspapers throughout the country were banned from serialising or reporting a book written by the former M15 agent, Peter Wright. It contained allegations that MI5 had tried to destabilise Harold Wilson's government. The book was written in Tasmania, and widely reported throughout the world. It was published in the United States where it sold an estimated half a million copies, and it had become freely available in Britain. But the government used the Act to prevent the British public knowing about the book's disturbing allegations through the media.

In America, Australia and Sweden, a journalist can pick up a telephone and often call directly to a senior civil servant handling the subject of interest. In Britain, the most one can expect is usually an evasive comment from a departmental Press Officer.

Both the Labour Party and the Alliance are now committed to introducing a Freedom of Information Bill and abolishing the Official Secrets Act. In 1988, the Conservative Government was forced to write its own Bill, after one of its own backbenchers introduced a Private Members Bill to abolish the Official Secrets Act. His Bill received wide support, but was quashed when the Conservatives ordered an unprecedented three line whip to vote it down. At the time of writing the Bill promised by the government has not been published.

The People and the Media

The recommendations made in 'The People and the Media' in 1974 were the basis of the Labour Party's evidence to both the Royal Commission on the Press and the Annan Committee on Broadcasting.

For the Press, it was agreed that reform would have to concentrate on a broad objective of tackling the monopolies by introducing competition and encouraging small circulation publications to cater for minority audiences who were not so attractive to advertisers. This would mean direct intervention by the government, unknown in Britain, but as we have seen, practised widely in other European countries.

The first proposal was for an Advertising Revenue Board which would try to remove the importance of advertising as a source of finance in newspapers. Then, as now, the proportion of revenue from advertising far outweighed the income from circulation and sales. Successful papers grow stronger because their larger sales attract the majority of advertising, while the weaker papers find it hard to compete. In the trade, so-called 'quality' newspapers like the *Times*, *Telegraph*, *Independent* and *Guardian* have comparatively low circulations, but their readers are generally well off, so they attract a lot of advertising. At the other end, 'popular' newspapers like the *Sun* and the *Mirror* attract high circulations, but generally their readers have low incomes, so there is not so much advertising. That means that only the popular papers with very large circulations can survive. A popular newspaper with an average circulation, and readers who are comparatively poor, cannot survive. The demise in 1964 of the *Daily Herald*, the former supporter of the Labour Party, was caused by having too many poor readers to attract advertising, even though its circulation was nearly two million. The *Times* sells only a fifth of that, yet it survives.

It was hoped that the new Board would shield the Press from the distortions of advertising finance. The Board would fix the advertising rates, collect the revenue and redistribute it back to the publications. Surplus profit would be retained in a special fund set up to subsidise newsprint, the paper used for printing, and to promote the launch of new publications. The Newsprint Subsidy was designed to encourage minority publications by removing the in-built advantages for the majority papers which could operate with huge economies of scale. The Launch Fund would make discretionary grants to new publications owned by non-profit making trusts. The main criteria for the grant, apart from availability of funds, was that the new publication should meet a need not already served, and should provide some sort of internal democracy for the workforce.

Other proposals were given less priority in the paper. These were the establishment of a National Printing Corporation, and a reform of the Press Council. As we have seen, the third Royal Commission did not advocate any of the measures in 'The People and the Media', though the minority report argued strongly for some degree of direct intervention in the Press.

The proposals for broadcasting, in contrast, were far more ambitious but less specific. In fact, they were so vague at times that it was never entirely clear whether the abolition of the BBC had been advocated or not. As usual the initial aims of the proposals were simple. They sought to encourage the growth of access to television and radio, and prevent both the existing authorities from becoming too large and institutionalised. It proposed two agencies; a Communications Council and a Public Broadcasting Commission.

The Communications Council had two functions; firstly to review the operation and development of new technology and to conduct research on the long-term policy implications. Secondly the Council would act as an Ombudsman in all complaints concerning television, radio and the Press (The Broadcasting Complaints Commission was later established following the report from the Annan Inquiry).

The other body was the Public Broadcasting Commission, which would be the overall funding agency for television and radio. It would collect advertising revenue and decide the level of other funding required from the public purse. The PBC would oversee the output of two television corporations, which both ran one network channel and one channel based on the output of the regions. It was hoped that this would encourage access from a wide range of 'programme units' (presumably production companies) from all parts of Britain. When it came to radio, the author seemed to run out of space. There was simply the sentence "There would be one or possibly two radio corporations. We see no future for commercial radio as such."

It is not surprising that such badly thought out proposals would receive short shrift from the Annan Committee. It takes very little knowledge to speculate that the thinly-veiled threat to abolish the BBC was in effect pressure from the Prime Minister, Harold Wilson, for the Corporation to 'toe the line'. It was public knowledge that he was still seething with indignation about the BBC programme titled *Yesterday's Men* which had attacked the previous Labour administration. Wilson was never regarded as being a friend of the BBC, and there were many private and public rows between his Cabinet and the Corporation. The point at issue was invariably 'anti-Labour' bias, which must be viewed ruefully in the 80's by old BBC hands battered by a stream of complaints from the Conservative Government.

Labour Proposals from 1980-83

The next serious attempt by the Labour Party to review media policy began in May 1980. The Media Committee, or Study Group, was chaired by the author of this book, Frank Allaun, and consisted of a wide range of trade unionists, MPs, journalists, television producers and academics. Its work was not completed when the election was called in June 1983.

The main proposal to emerge from the discussions was the establishment of an Open (or Independent) Press Authority. It was felt that only an independent body would be able to undertake the sort of radical proposals which the Committee had in mind. In essence, the Committee wanted the Government to set up a new structure for the Press which would not be seen as direct intervention, because it would be administered by a separate body. The IPA would be a public agency, subject to Parliament, but composed of representatives of all political parties, the public and the unions. Eventually it would operate like the Independent Broadcasting Authority and award franchises to groups to run newspapers. In broadcasting, of course, the number of franchises is limited by the number of airwaves available and the spread of the different regions. For newspapers, the only limit on the number of franchises would be the capacity of an area to support a range of publications. Newspaper groups with too large a monopoly would have to 'disinvest' or sell off some of their titles and a fund would be established to encourage new publications and support ailing ones.

The franchises would last for seven years and would permit proprietors to run enough provincial or local papers to make each group viable. Not more than one daily and one Sunday paper would be desirable for each group. Two other conditions would possibly go with the franchise: one, that newspaper franchises should not be awarded to groups who had substantial proven assets in television and radio; secondly, and more controversially, that a franchise would only be awarded if the publications involved were run either as trusts, or as co-operatives.

The IPA would obviously have to administer some major changes before the franchise system would work. The worst problem, as far as the study group was concerned, was the failure of the anti-monopoly legislation, already outlined in Chapter 3. The reason that the legislation had failed is that amalgamation is often the only answer to impending closure. If there was a safety net, or a separate fund, many of the publications could have been relaunched as public trusts. The main groups are now so powerful that if further take-overs were prohibited it would be like shutting the stable door after the horse had bolted. It was suggested that newspaper groups with circulations totalling nine million or over should be broken up. At present this would only affect Rupert Murdoch and Robert Maxwell. Murdoch would have to sell the *Times* and *Sunday Times*, while Maxwell would have to sell the *Sunday Mirror* or the *Sunday People*. A separate figure would be set for provincial newspaper conglomerates.

The other major problem was how to decide the criteria on which newspapers would receive help from the IPA, either to prevent a closure, or to launch a new paper onto the market. The general view was that a launch fund should begin to help new papers only after they had proved there was a demand for them, and had already secured a sale of say, fifty thousand. Aid would be discontinued after the papers reached a figure of up to a million copies a day. This proposal essentially rejects the system of political support in Sweden (Chapter 5), and concurs with the scheme put forward in the Minority Report of the third Royal Commission (Chapter 4). The finance would come from two sources: the majority from a tax on advertising, and the rest from the government. Its main aim would be to correct the distortion that advertising has on newspaper economics, and the grants would be awarded accordingly. They would either be calculated on a ratio between sales and advertising: the fewer adverts, the higher the grant. Alternatively, it would be according to the proportion of editorial matter to advertising matter.

Three other matters on the Press were considered by the Working Group. It was agreed that the law on distribution should be changed to bring it into line with the French system, and that a National Printing Corporation should be considered. Both these reforms were thought to be of minor importance by some of the contributors. The wholesalers generally take most publications with a sizeable circulation, they argued, and there is plenty of spare printing capacity in the country for groups who want to start new publications.

There was general distaste about the growing trend of paying for stories by cheque-book journalism, many of which were salacious and offensive to large sections of the public. It was suggested that newspapers should be required by law to state at the beginning or end of a news item if they had entered into an agreement to pay for the story. (This was also raised in 1986 in Parliament in an unsuccessful Private Members Bill. It is now generally recognised that the Press Council is unable to prevent the spread of cheque-book journalism).

The majority of these proposals were still in discussion when the General Election of 1983 was called. Consequently they were not agreed even by the Media Committee, let alone by the National Executive of the Labour Party. Two members of the group were particularly opposed to some of the more radical ideas. They held that the introduction of more controls over the media was not the way to safeguard the public against distortion, manipulation or concentration of ownership. "We must encourage diversity of sources and of editorial inputs", they argued. "Proposals to democratise the media by other means might produce the real danger of making the Press more inhibited and cowardly. It is difficult to tackle these problems... without generating public hostility and running into acute problems over the freedom of the press." Instead, they advocated that the Labour Party should make sure that it allows the proper use of the technical developments, not only in newspaper production, but in the areas of broadcasting where change was rapid: local radio, off-air television, and cable and satellite television. In the event, discussions over these crucial areas were also incomplete, and since 1983, many of the expected developments have taken place.

The most coherent approach to broadcasting came from three television producers who argued strongly for a dramatic deregulation of the BBC and the IBA. They said that television and radio were intent on reflecting the views of the 'consensus' in society by acting in an 'impartial' way. "But who determines what is impartial?" they asked. "Usually the BBC and IBA". They said it was wrong to believe that there was such a thing as impartiality. What the broadcasters should be doing is reflecting not the consensus, but the variety or plurality in society.

Their plan was to remove both the BBC and IBA from having total control over broadcasting. The BBC, they said, was monolithic and centralised; and ITV was too profit-oriented. Instead they wanted more democratic control over broadcasting organisations, and more access to the airwaves for under-represented groups. In the same way as 'The People and the Media' in 1974, they saw the breaking up of the BBC and IBA and the creation of two new bodies. The first would be the National Communications Authority. Its functions would be to collect revenue in the present form of advertising money, licence fees and government income, and redistribute it to the companies involved, in proportion to the nature and quantity of their output. It would allocate contracts and franchises for organisations, allocate frequencies, and co-ordinate policy between separate companies. The other body would be a separate unit known as the National Communications Council, which would act as a watchdog on the NCA, monitor its performance and adjudicate complaints. Both bodies would include a majority of members who had been elected onto Regional Communications Councils.

These proposals were so far-reaching that it is not surprising that not only did they attract opposition within the study group, but they also ran out of time. In the end the 1983 Labour Party manifesto contained some strong generalities, but few specific plans. Here it is:

Labour Manifesto on the Media 1983
"Our aims in the media are to safeguard freedom of expression, encourage diversity and establish greater accountability. For all the media, we will introduce a statutory right of reply to ensure that individuals can set the record straight. We will introduce stronger measures to prevent any further concentration in the media.

For the Press, we will encourage diversity by: setting up a launch fund to assist new publications; ensuring that all major wholesalers accept any lawful publication, and arrange for its proper supply and display, subject to a handling charge; preventing acquisition of further newspapers by large Press chains; protecting freedom of expression by prohibiting joint control of the Press, commercial radio and television; breaking up major concentrations of press ownership, by setting an upper limit for the number of major publications in the hands of a single proprietor or press group; replacing the Press Council with a stronger, more representative body.

In broadcasting, we will aim to make both broadcasting itself, and the organisations responsible, more accountable and representative, and to provide greater public access. Our aim is to promote a more wide-ranging and genuine pluralism in the media, as we set out in our proposals in Labour's Programme in 1982. We will also seek to introduce a genuinely independent adjudication of grievances and complaints. The licence fee will be phased out for pensioners during the lifetime of the Labour Government.

The high standards of British public service broadcasting are threatened by Tory plans to introduce cable TV on free-market principles. We will regulate satellite and cable provision, and foster the same principles of diversity and pluralism as conventional broadcasting authorities. To avoid wasteful duplication, we will entrust the provision of the national cable system to British Telecom."

During the four years between 1983 and 1987 little was done specifically on newspapers, radio and television within the Labour Party. The shadow Minister of Arts established a forum called 'Arts for Labour' which considered some aspects previously covered in depth by the Media Committee. The biggest controversy occurred within the Party in the run-up to the election. The plan put forward by the group was for the BBC to be put under the control of a new Ministry for the Arts and Media. This was resisted by some senior members of the shadow Cabinet, and it was eventually decided that it should stay under the control of the Home Office — a rather ambiguous position. The 1987 Election manifesto was shorter, and like the 1983, consisted mostly of generalities.

> "We will establish a Ministry for the Arts and Media with responsibility for the arts, crafts, public libraries, museums, film, publishing, the press, the record industry, the development of broadcasting and access to it, fashion, design, architecture and the heritage. The Home Office will remain responsible for regulatory and statutory powers in relation to broadcasting.
>
> The development of central and local government support for the arts, culture and entertainment is essential to the extension of choice, access and participation, and to the development of the related industries.
>
> We will protect the independence of the BBC and the independent broadcasting organisations. We reject subscription television for the BBC and the auctioning of ITV franchises.
>
> We will legislate to ensure that ownership and control of the press and broadcasting media are retained by citizens of Britain and to place limits on the concentration of ownership. We will strengthen the Press Council and set up a launch fund to assist new publications in order to encourage the diversity necessary in a healthy democracy."

The major difference between the 1983 Manifesto and the 1987 one, was that the latter had no mention of a statutory right of reply. And despite all the evidence against the Press Council over the years, the Labour Party was showing signs of returning to a policy of shoring-up the much discredited complaints body.

The Right of Reply

> "For all the media, we will introduce a statutory right of reply to ensure that individuals can set the record straight."

The 1983 Manifesto's commitment to the Right of Reply was unequivocal. The author of this book had already presented a Right of Reply Bill to Parliament on three occasions, and it had steadily increased support from MPs of all parties. Over ten other countries already have adopted similar measures, and we saw in Chapter Four how it works in France and Germany. We have also seen the failure of the Press Council (Chapter 3) to control the worst excesses of newspapers.

Critics of the right of reply argue that there is already a suitable response to defamation and that is in the civil courts. Taking a libel action, however, is an expensive and time-consuming business, usually taking over eighteen months to come to court. If successful, of course, it can reap immense dividends for those defamed. But the expense of employing a solicitor and barrister makes it a solution only for those with considerable financial resources. It is not possible to get legal aid for libel actions, and consequently the weight of the law is biased in favour of those who can afford it. It will not stop millionaires like Sir James Goldsmith from suing *Private Eye*, but it can stop individuals from taking effective action.

There have been five attempts by backbench Labour MPs to introduce a Bill on right of reply. The first three were introduced by Frank Allaun. Then there was an attempt by Austin Mitchell, and in 1988, there was a further attempt by Ann Clwyd.

The original Allaun Bill would give an individual, organisation or company the right to require the editor of a newspaper, which has carried a factually inaccurate report involving themselves, to print a reply within three days. The reply would have to be printed free of charge, and be of equal length to the offending part of the original article, and in the same position and type, however prominent. If the editor refuses, after three days the case would go to a tribunal with a judge as chairman, which must make a judgement within three days. If the complainant's right of reply is upheld the editor would be required to print it immediately, and also pay a fine of up to £40,000 (as in France). In election periods, the three day limit would be reduced to 24 hours for daily newspapers. For periodicals, it would have to appear in the next issue. The same right would apply where there has been a misrepresentation of fact on television or radio. The existing libel law would remain unchanged.

Ann Clwyd's Bill was similar to the earlier ones. Called the Unfair Reporting and Right of Reply Bill, it never reached a second reading. Like the previous Bills it gave people the right to correct inaccuracies. But instead of a Tribunal, the Bill proposed the establishment of a Media Commission with the legal authority to require publication of corrections. This Commission would be comprised of 21 members appointed by the Secretary of State. It would monitor media standards, issuing guidelines where necessary, and make an annual report to Parliament. The Bill also went a stage further on the question of libel. It was proposed that legal aid would be extended to include civil actions for defamation.

Each time the question of the right of reply is raised in Parliament it has encouraged debate about standards in the media. For many MPs, both Conservative and Labour, those standards have never been so low. But while there is a majority Conservative Government, it is unlikely that such a Bill would be passed. After all, the Press do not like it, and the majority of the Press support the Conservative Party.

To the average person in the street, a right of reply to an inaccuracy is merely logical and just. Its simplicity and commonsense makes it potentially a very popular form of reform in the media. There are no massive changes in the structure of newspapers, radio and television; just the right for a wronged person to be heard.

The experience overseas is that the right of reply is not abused. But nobody knows how far its very existence prevents papers from indulging in the excesses that have been experienced in Britain.

There was widespread opposition among the papers when the Bills were presented to Parliament. There were predictable claims that it would interfere in the freedom of the press, and that it would impose a belated censorship on newspapers. There have also been some more informed criticisms which are relevant.

Lord Ardwick, the former editor of the *Daily Herald*, wrote in *The Independent* against the Bill, and particularly the extension of legal aid to libel actions. "It would open the floodgates not only to the poor afflicted ones who write in green ink, but also the propagandists, the conviction politicians, the animal lovers, the anti-polluters and so on. They are already a heavy burden and the provision of finance for libel actions would add to it."

Other worries are expressed by investigative reporters in both television and newspapers. They fear that its application could be used by senior public figures and large corporations to stop revealing stories being run on them. In television especially, the complications of providing a full right of reply to, say, a half hour investigative documentary is something which has not been fully considered. This argument accepts that some newspapers have a bad track record, and that some people have no proper recourse. The question is where to strike the balance between inhibiting journalistic inquiry, and protecting innocent individuals from the inaccuracies and smears of the popular Press. In television, programme makers are already restricted by the BBC and IBA guidelines, as well as the time consuming response to the Broadcasting Complaints Commission.

In newspapers, these reservations have been best expressed to me by Paul Foot, an investigative reporter on the *Daily Mirror*.

"I am against the right of reply. From my experience of regulatory bodies which exist outside the trade union movement, the Press Council is the best example, it seems to be quite clear that such bodies are used in the main by the powerful against those few occasions in the Press where the powerful are rumbled."

"The right of reply would almost certainly be used to my disadvantage over and over again, by the people I am attacking. I am at the moment able to beat off attacks, both if they come on the legal front, and if they came in letters to the Editor, simply by pointing out that they are unjustified. A regulatory body, enforcing a right of reply would, in my view, not take the same view as the editor or the lawyer here, (at the *Daily Mirror*) and as a result the few criticisms I am able to make of society would be quickly rubbed out by the great and powerful exercising their right of reply."

He adds:

"I would rather have the Press Council than nothing, to be honest... I should have thought that society is littered with the impotent or dead bodies of regulatory organisations set up by Labour Governments."

Even its supporters agree that the right of reply is no panacea. It does not deal with what many see as the media's main failing, which is often not a question of telling lies, but the deliberate and biased selection of news. The only way to counter that is to make sure that bias in one direction is matched by other publications which are partisan in the other direction. But while there is a Press which is owned by a narrow band of opinion formers, there is no immediate cure.

The question for the right of reply is where to strike the balance. Are the justified claims of wronged individuals more important than the encouragement of inquiring journalism? Are people over-exaggerating the impact of a right of reply, or could it inhibit the very kind of journalism that many of its proposers want to encourage? These questions are considered in more detail in the last chapter.

CHAPTER NINE

Towards Reform

The last ten years have altered the shape of the British Press.

It has witnessed a decline in standards in the popular papers so profound that it is difficult to know how the position can be reversed under the present system. There is more sensationalism, more political bias, more trivia, and worst of all, there are more inaccuracies and lies. And yet, for many, the political changes in Britain at the moment require more scrutiny, more explanation and more opposition among the Press than ever before. They say that the British Press is letting down our parliamentary democracy.

So is it time for a government of any political persuasion to tackle the distortions in the structure of the media? The Conservative Government in 1988 issued a strong warning to newspapers about the abuse of the Press Council, and threatened to replace self-regulating machinery with statutory controls. Few saw this as more than a gesture to those MPs who had supported the Right of Reply Bills. And as the former editor of the *Daily Telegraph*, Lord Deedes, has said "Mrs Thatcher will never act against newspapers."

So the most likely candidate for the job would be an incoming Labour administration. They have most to complain about and most to gain by encouraging a more representative Press. But past Labour governments have refused to clutch the nettle, no doubt because Cabinet Ministers were nervous about spoiling their finely tuned relationships with the media. In the past, Labour administrations have always found reasons to dodge any serious reform.

Today there are new reasons which can be used as an excuse to do nothing. Some people argue that the so-called 'revolution in Fleet Street' will lead to a wider diversity of newspapers, without the tedious and controversial legislation needed to otherwise encourage it. There are others who say that the Press industry has lost its importance compared to the huge growth in the variety of broadcasting media; that video, satellite and cable will soon become more important than the printed word.

Future governments would be wrong if they ignored the Press because of these developments. The revolution in Fleet Street has raised more questions about control in papers, not less. Yet, at the same time, it means that the time is right for using it to encourage proper diversity of the Press. This will not happen on its own without some encouragement. It is feared that without such stimulation, the technological revolution will just produce more of the same, without leading to a new variety of differing newspapers and magazines. As for its relative importance compared to broadcasting, nobody should underestimate the partisan reporting of the Press in 'setting the agenda' for the more neutral television and radio stations. Neither should people forget the appalling depths to which parts of our newspaper industry have sunk over the last ten years and the inability of the Press Council to do anything about it.

In December 1987, Sir Zelman Cowen of the Press Council warned that newspapers which treat their rulings cynically were putting themselves at risk of more profound sanctions. "If newspapers persist in such behaviour they will surely jeopardise the future of self-control of British newspapers", he said. The patience of many seems to have already run out, and they want action. It is not surprising that there has been growing support for a statutory Right of Reply.

Up to now, successive British governments have prided themselves on having no policy on the Press. They have seen legislation on the Press as smacking of interference in the free spread of information, an invitation to an Orwellian future where newspaper headlines are written by the Ministry of Truth. This belief seems hypocritical when it is considered how many times Parliament has debated Broadcasting Bills which put wide restrictions on the ownership of television and radio. Now indeed a Broadcasting Standards Council is to be established by statute, which if anything, could be described as being truly Orwellian.

European governments do not have the same preoccupation with such literary predictions. They believe that they have taken steps to safeguard the freedom of the media by using some of the ideas which we in Britain have been shy about. They say that few people have complained that these measures have stopped the Press from carrying out its proper functions.

This book has not set out to give firm answers to the questions that it has posed. But we have tried to show the range of ideas which are available to those who wish to reform the Press. There is one conclusion which comes from nearly all the proposals that we consider: some sort of legislation, or Press Bill, will be necessary if such ideas are to be put into action. In the past, such a proposition was enough to send editors reaching for their books of quotations. The most popular choice would be the famous saying of William Pitt in the House of Commons in 1783:

> "Necessity is the plea for every infringement of human freedom. It is the argument of tyrants; it is the creed of slaves."

Yet if such legislation is framed properly, then its proposers argue that it will not infringe human rights and will not be aimed at editors. It will seek to give editors more, not less, freedom of operation. It is well recognised that they need to be emancipated from both legal restrictions and proprietorial ones. Only then, it is argued, will they be able to perform the important social function that a free Press demands. Any measure which has the direct, or indirect, effect of restricting journalists from having the right to report, to enquire or campaign, would be rejected, they say.

What should such legislation seek to achieve? Over the years, as we have seen, many ideas have been floated, and usually rejected by the three Royal Commissions on the industry. To get an up-to-date view of current thinking, we have looked at the opinions of three people who have a long track record in supporting reform of the media.

The Meacher Plan

Michael Meacher MP has played a leading role in shaping Labour policy and many of his ideas were included in the 1983 Manifesto. He supports the introduction of a right of reply and the establishment of an Advertising Revenue Board. This would distribute advertising in a way which would offset the need for some publications to rely on it as a source of survival. A percentage of the advertising would go into a fund, topped up with government money, which would assist the launch of new publications, prevent the closure of old ones, subsidise newsprint and possibly create a National Printing Corporation. He argues that government intervention confined to economic action of this kind does not encroach upon the freedom of the press. He cites an academic study by Anthony Smith of the academic study group, 'Political Economic Planning', on subsidies in Europe, in which it is shown that in practice they do not influence editorial policy.

He goes on to call for the replacement of the Press Council with an Independent Press Authority with functions similar to the IBA in broadcasting. He says that the IPA should award franchises to the existing national press for a seven year period on condition that they keep to a Code of Standards drawn up by the authority. If the paper was judged to have fallen short of the standards, it would lose the franchise. Other proposals included a statutory right of distribution, along French lines, and shifting government responsibility for the media into a new Ministry for the Arts, Communications and Entertainment. He argues that the fragmentation of ministerial and departmental responsibility has been an excuse for inaction. At present the Department of Trade and Industry, and the Home Office, both have responsibility for parts of the media. Meacher proposes that the new Ministry would be headed by a Secretary of State with a place in the Cabinet, whose function would be to provide a "balanced, diverse and pluralistic media which would be designed to avoid both any degree of state control over editorial content, and the domination of private market criteria by tycoons and multi-national corporations." It would be the Ministry responsible for the BBC, ITV, IBA, national and regional press, the new Independent Press Authority, the Advertising Revenue Board, State subsidies for the economics of the Press, the new national distribution systems and the development of information technology, which would include cable and satellite.

The Curran Plan
James Curran is an academic and journalist, who was the first editor of *New Socialist*, the bi-monthly magazine of the Labour Party. Much of his analysis criticises previous Labour governments for their failure to tackle reform of the Press. "Press policy in Britain has long been based on the conservative principle that it is best to have no policy at all."

Curran believes that the role of television is also important, and his proposals encompass the need to tackle not only newspapers, but also the growth of global communications conglomerates which now reach around the world. To stop the threat of 'global media moguls' like Murdoch, he proposed three anti-monopoly measures:

1. No group or individual should be allowed to own more than three national newspapers or more than ten local daily papers, or more than 50 local weekly (paid or freesheet) papers within the United Kingdom.

2. No group or individual should be allowed to own over 10% of shares in more than one ITV company or franchised cable TV company or local radio company.

3. No group or individual should be allowed to own voting shares in both Press and broadcasting organisations.

He expects that many conglomerates would have to sell off part of their operation as a consequence. Curran proposes that a Media Enterprise Board should be established to buy up some of these spare concerns and launch new media. It would be financed directly from the Exchequer which would impose a tax on all advertising to pay for it.

In addition to this, Curran seeks wider access to the media market by advocating the legal right to distribution and new grants for papers struggling to attract advertising. In broadcasting, the IBA and the new Cable TV Authority should give some franchises to non-profit making organisations. There should be a restriction on the number of imported programmes shown on cable and satellite (DBS) television, and a better social mix of representatives to the Boards of the BBC, IBA, Channel Four and the Cable TV Authority. All this would go hand in hand with a Freedom of Information Act and the abolition of the Official Secrets Act.

The Baistow Plan
Tom Baistow is a distinguished journalist whose long-standing

concern about the declining standards of the Press led him to mastermind the drawing up of the Right of Reply Bill.

He argues that part of the blame for the current state of the Press should lie with the print unions in Fleet Street who forced unreasonable agreements on weak management. This emphasis is associated with a hope that the new era of electronic publishing, with realistic union agreements, could in the long term "bring about a gradual return to the diversity essential to an informed, socially balanced and politically literate democracy."

Baistow goes on to call for a comprehensive Press Law or Charter which would map out responsibilities on libel and contempt laws, freedom of information, right of reply and invasion of privacy. It would also establish a legal framework for some basic changes.

(a) All takeover bids should be referred to the Monopolies Commission, which must give special consideration to bids by consortia of editorial staff and management. Ownership and control of newspapers should be restricted to persons of British nationality, and companies whose headquarters are registered in the UK.

(b) The reform of the Press Council so that it has powers to fine offenders for breaches of a new Code of Conduct based on the existing NUJ code.

(c) Each national newspaper should appoint an ombudsman to settle routine complaints from the public.

(d) Each national newspaper would have independent directors appointed to them who would have to approve the engagement or dismissal of editors. Editorial staff should be legally entitled to have a say in the appointment of editors.

(e) The introduction of the right of distribution.

The provisions of the Press Law would be overseen by an Independent Press Authority, along the lines of the Independent Broadcasting Authority.

All three plans raise fundamental questions about the long-term development of the media in Britain. They provide the background to a debate which has been going on for forty years and which may still hold the key to future reform. The most recent model for debate has come from the Campaign for Press and Broadcasting Freedom. They have produced a 'Media Manifesto', which is designed to stimulate debate around the subject of reform. They have held meetings and conferences to explain the measures that they propose, and to get feedback on the ideas. From this they produced a draft resolution for unions and other organisations to consider:

Draft Resolution
The purpose of the resolution is to campaign for a programme of reform to

ensure greater access to and democratic accountability in the media, including:

(a) Freedom of Information legislation, the repeal of the Official Secrets Act and the Prevention of Terrorism Act; reform of the Contempt of Court Act to allow full coverage of the administration of justice; an end to security vetting in broadcasting; and the abolition of the D-notice and Parliamentary Lobby systems.

(b) legislation to restrict the number of publications and media outlets owned by any one company or group of companies, and to halt the concentration of ownership in the electronic media.

(c) the establishment of an integrated Ministry of Broadcasting, Arts and Telecommunications;

(d) revision of broadcasting legislation to ensure elected, representative bodies replace the existing system of appointment to the IBA and the BBC Board of Governors, and the creation of accountable regional Media Councils responsible for the allocation and supervision of TV, radio, cable and satellite franchises;

(e) the provision of accessible media facilities through the establishment of a National Printing Corporation and regional Media Enterprise Boards able to invest in new publishing and broadcasting projects and promote training, funded from a levy on all media advertising, taxation and local authority grant;

(f) bringing British Telecom back under public control and establishing an elected National Telecommunications Council with power to ensure that new technologies (including satellite and cable) are developed first and foremost as a public service, and to regulate international satellite transmissions in co-operation with other countries.

(g) an obligation on all media institutions to publicise and uphold a Code of Conduct covering professional ethics, and to guarantee space for a broad range of opinions on matters of industrial, social and political importance; and the creation of advisory bodies to monitor matters of representation relating to class, sexuality, race and disability in terms of both output and employment.

(h) a Statutory Right of Reply;

(i) legislation to guarantee distribution and display of all legitimate publications;

(j) the introduction of forms of industrial democracy that allow media workers direct involvement in editorial and managerial decision making.

The resolution is obviously far-reaching and contains many of the ideas already put forward in earlier chapters. Some of the ideas are impractical given the present political realities. If by some chance it was enacted it would take up much parliamentary time, but if just some of the proposals were to come into force then it may just help rescue the Press from the pit into which it has fallen.

Summary

Reform of the media will always be controversial, and some of the ideas expressed in this book would be unsatisfactory even to some of those who see the need for change. However, enough has been said to show that some reform of the media, particularly the Press, is not only desirable but beneficial to maintaining a true parliamentary democracy. In this final section I summarise some of the points that have been made and assess their worth.

Broadcasting

Despite a growing body of research into broadcasting, there is little broad agreement about which are the major problems and how they should be tackled. The debate about the future of the BBC is one example. There are strong criticisms to be made about the Corporation's size, its centralised system of control, its funding, its middle-class staff bias and its quasi-independent relationship with the Government. But equally, in the face of cable and satellite, there are strong arguments for maintaining a sizeable public service sector as a way of preventing a drift into poorer quality broadcasting. As the NUJ submission to the Peacock Committee said:

> "It is a system which strikes a delicate balance between the public and commercial interest. It is admired, envied and emulated abroad. It is a system which has helped to nourish innovation and development in drama, documentary, music, news, current affairs, entertainment, comedy and numerous other fields."

The Conservative Government is to respond to the Peacock Committee with a Broadcasting Bill, making changes in radio and the way that franchises are awarded to the commercial companies.

The most profound attack on the quality of our broadcasting system could turn out to be in the independent sector. Early in 1988 'government sources' suggested that the Cabinet committee on broadcasting had decided that the sixteen ITV franchises would be "auctioned" to the highest bidder when they came up for renewal in 1992. The Committee was chaired by the Prime Minister herself, and reflected her strong belief that free market forces should be introduced into radio and television, as occurs in the United States.

But the critics of such a policy say it will lead to the low standards of American television, with each network fighting for audiences by transmitting low-brow games shows, situation comedies and police thrillers. Quality drama, documentaries and current affairs are conspicuously absent from the schedules of unregulated, free-market television.

If the ITV franchises are to be awarded to the highest bidder in 1992, it could mean that the companies will be forced to copy the American networks. Large audiences mean higher revenue from advertising. Games shows and comedies are cheap to make compared to drama and documentaries, and get larger audiences. A company pursuing an American schedule could afford to bid more than a company which has committed itself to making higher quality programmes. If the commercial companies have to follow the former course, the delicate balance with the BBC will be lost, and so might Britain's reputation as having the best television in the world.

So overall, significant changes to the existing structure of broadcasting need to be considered with care. The other area of future concern is in the cable and satellite fields, and any future governments should put a great deal of energy into assessing the long-term significance of these developments now that a pattern is beginning to emerge. How important is the concentration of ownership in the hands of Murdoch, Maxwell and the other existing media conglomerates? Should we be worried about Ted Turner's world-wide news service and its threat of a new brand of cultural imperialism? Who will regulate the satellites hundreds of miles away in space, oblivious of British laws of obscenity and libel? These questions need to be considered well before there is any easy reform of broadcasting.

The Labour Party has already said it would remove advertising and sponsorship on the BBC if it was imposed. The Alliance are also against advertising on the BBC. But both parties agree that a licence fee needs reviewing as a form of funding and that the BBC needs to be more accountable.

It is argued by many that the BBC Board of Governors has become less representative since 1979 because of the large number of apparently political appointments made by the Conservative Government. One way to diffuse such a position would be temporarily to enlarge the Board by appointing an extra group of Governors to cancel out those which are deemed to have been selected for political purposes. This could be a short-term measure until a more satisfactory form of funding and control could be devised for the BBC.

The Press
(1) The Right of Reply
There is increasing consensus that a law on the right of reply is the only way of hitting back at an industry which has consistently failed to

police itself. The public is becoming more aware of the political bias, sensationalism, poor reporting and triviality of a Press which is supposed to provide information, intelligent comment and inquiring journalism. The newspaper industry should not be surprised that pressure for a right of reply is intensifying. It only has itself to blame for that.

The supporters of the right of reply know it is no panacea. It runs the risk of being used in a mischievous way to stifle the sort of investigative journalism that most people appreciate. But there is now no option to a measure designed to curb the worst excesses of an industry which has lost its morality. Britain's Press industry has failed consistently to regulate itself, and there is no reason to think that they will begin to do so now. Yet the experience of other countries suggests that the right of reply does not lead to excessive pressure on editors, and in fact it appears to promote the very self-regulation which the Press Council in Britain has been unable to maintain.

The right of reply on its own, however, is not going to establish a free Press. It is likely that, in order to achieve the aims put forward by reformers, a future government will have to pass a Press Bill. The proposals for such a Bill should not be designed to add constraints to editors, or to prevent partisan journalism. Partisan journalism has provided the sort of informed comment which has led to great changes in our society over the years. But readers at least expect that informed comment is based on the facts necessary to prove the argument. Nobody should dispute the right of papers like the *Sun* to exist, only that it has standards and it has competition. A reforming Press Bill is seen as the obvious way to encourage both.

(2) The lifting of legal constraints
At the moment, editors are prevented from following the finest traditions of journalism by the existence of a large number of legal constraints. They want to be able to report court cases without unwarranted hindrance, to be able to bring to account people in public service who they believe are abusing their position, and they want to have the informed knowledge to be able to assess a government's record in office. Press legislation could set down the right of a journalist not to reveal the source of published or unpublished information. It could make amendments to the Contempt of Court Act, and the Police and Criminal Evidence Act. It could introduce a proper Freedom of Information Act.

Such measures would play a big part in encouraging inquiring journalism across all newspapers. At present, investigative reporting is rare because it is so expensive compared to the relatively modest increase in circulation that can be expected from pursuing such stories. It would become less expensive to do serious journalism if the information required was relatively easy to gather. The role of the media as a 'public watchdog' would be greatly enhanced.

(3) Anti-monopoly measures

It has long been recognised that the present anti-monopoly legislation is not strong enough to prevent further concentration within the Press industry. For most people, it has already gone far enough, and it would be wrong just to introduce tough measures which would merely leave the situation as it stands. There are strong arguments for splitting up some of the present Press conglomerates. Similar legislation in West Germany, France and the United States show that it is not such a radical move.

Such a law could restrict any one company from holding a controlling interest in more than one national daily and one Sunday newspaper. Similar restrictions could be placed on regional morning and evening newspapers and weeklies, including freesheets. In the past it would have been argued that newspaper groups have to have a spread of titles to be profitable. But the present state of newspapers shows this to be untrue. If the *Telegraph*, *Guardian*, *Observer* and *Independent* can survive, there is no reason why titles within the Murdoch or Maxwell chains could not prosper within smaller groups. The onset of new technology in the Press only serves to strengthen this position. The legislation could permit groups which had to disinvest themselves of titles to lease out the spare printing capacity to the new owners.

The legislation might also follow the Australian and American model in restricting ownership across all types of media: newspapers, television and radio. This would ensure that the country, and each region, could enjoy some plurality in its media.

(4) Ministry for the Arts and Communications

The increasing amount of leisure time and the wide expansion of broadcasting suggests that there is some substance in the Labour Party's proposals for a Ministry for Arts and Communications. If it was to have any real power it would also have to have the BBC and IBA within its responsibility. A break from the Home Office into a Ministry more sympathetic to the nature of broadcasting would probably be welcomed.

It would also be in a position to oversee the changes in the Press. It could appoint an Independent Press Authority which would have responsibility for seeing through the changes which would have to be made following any anti-monopoly legislation. It would also have responsibility for setting and maintaining standards. It could be financed jointly from the industry and government, and consist of representatives of the proprietors, the trade unions and selected independent individuals.

The IPA would also be in a position to abandon the Press Council and appoint a Media Commission or Ombudsman to provide a well staffed office to adjudicate complaints from the public. Its main role would be to make sure that the Right of Reply legislation was being adhered to by the media. This office could also have the power to fine offending newspapers and order them to carry a statement, similar in size to the original article, to put the facts straight.

The Commission could also have the power to advise newspapers and journalists on the right of privacy for individuals, except where it could be shown that the scrutiny of public affairs is in the public interest. One other function could be the encouragement of self-financing training facilities to promote the highest standards of journalism.

(5) Launching new publications

The Independent Press Authority could also play an important role in helping new publications to become viable. First it would put a statutory duty on retailers to display publications. Distributors and retailers would still be liable to prosecution under the obscenity laws, but could be exempted from civil libel actions.

Secondly, the IPA would have to do something to tackle the inequitable balance between revenue from advertising and circulation that threatens the viability of so many newspapers early in their life. The main proposal from the Labour Party, the Advertising Revenue Board, would to many people intervene to an unacceptable degree in the commercial life of newspapers. It would also put their profitability into the hands of other people and raise suspicions of political patronage and editorial interference.

. Instead, the IPA could administrate a system of providing grants or long-term loans to new newspapers, or companies willing to take-over titles disinvested by anti-monopoly legislation. In the past this would have been impractical because of the high costs involved, but the lower margins of new technology now bring such a system into the scope of government action. It is not as if a large number of new publications would start clamouring for government money, because there is still a huge minimum investment necessary for such projects. *News On Sunday*, for instance, needed £7 million pounds to launch the publication. The problem was finding the finance to keep going while finding its feet. What the IPA could do over a set period is make grants or loans available to publications, paying them according to a cost curve analysis related to circulation and distribution. If, for instance, *News On Sunday* had had an extra million pounds in its first year, it would probably still be publishing today. Given the fact that this would apply to only a small number of papers, it is a small cost to pay for a democratic Press. After all, the Exchequer made £63 million pounds in 1986/7 from its levy on the advertising sold by the ITV companies.In addition, VAT is now being charged on advertisements in newspapers, another source of considerable revenue for the Exchequer from the media industry. What is being proposed is a fraction of the money given to the government each year by the media, on top of their normal taxes.

Of course, the whole point of the exercise is to encourage the sort of newspapers which are under-represented at the moment in our national Press. How would the IPA prevent a semi-pornographic paper like the *Sunday Sport* from applying for help? The answer is simple. The grants or loans would only be available to publications which fulfilled the criteria of what most people recognise as responsible journalism. The IPA could be responsible for drawing up an ideal model for ownership.

(6) An ownership model

Such a model might include a commitment to encourage industrial democracy in the structure of their organisations. Newspapers play such a pivotal role in influencing the public's perception of events, that most people would feel that it is desirable for them to be run by a broader cross section of society than just one man — the proprietor. For instance, the IPA might insist that all major appointments and policy decisions are referred to a Board of which 40% are elected from the workforce, 40% are shareholders and the other 20% are independent directors appointed by the Press authority. This would give them some say in the way that their own investment is being managed. They could also insist that the existing journalists' Code of Conduct is adopted as a working model by the newspaper. Again it might be possible to limit the allocation of grants or loans to companies which are British-owned. This would provide a useful tool to counteract the disturbing number of foreign owners in our Press, without taking the somewhat racist measure of banning them completely. After all, few people would want a situation, which could easily develop under the present system, where all our national newspapers were owned by proprietors from overseas.

At the same time, industrial democracy should not seek to introduce a collective approach to editorial decision making. The experience of *News On Sunday*, and the *Scottish Daily News*, shows that an editor must have the right to make decisions. That is not to say that the editor is not accountable, it merely means that policy is not being discussed from issue to issue. It should be considered over a period of time.

Such a proposal would not interfere with the existing Press. Many newspaper owners would not appreciate the intrusion of a model of industrial democracy, and would therefore not take up the chance of applying for grants. But the papers which could not survive on their own, and which do not have huge commercial enterprises behind them, would be encouraged. The advantage of such a scheme is that it enhances Press freedom without removing the right of any person to run a newspaper for profit in the way they see fit.

The anti-monopoly measures would limit the number of titles that a proprietor may hold, and a system of awarding grants would insist on certain standards of journalism. Given the sad loss of morality in the industry over the last ten years, these are conditions that many people will support. At the moment there is a technological revolution in our Press which gives us a realistic chance of reforming the industry. But the presence of new technology on its own is not enough to bring a new diversity; so far it has only given us more of the same. It should be harnessed to, and promoted to, take us that stage further. It cannot be done without some form of legislation. But the encouragement of new newspapers is the only way of achieving a truly democratic representation in our Press.

What Now?

None of the proposals described in this book is going to happen tomorrow. There will be a long wait before the industry is changed for the better. So what should be done now? There is only one course to take, and that is to continue to expose the existing system so that eventually the case for reform becomes so overwhelming that something has to be done.

Thirty years ago it was said in Fleet Street that dog doesn't eat dog. Newspapers hardly ever drew attention to the wrongdoings of their rivals. That attitude has changed somewhat today, and it should be encouraged, if only because newspapers who are throwing stones have to make sure they are not themselves living in glass houses.

Readers should not allow themselves to put up with the excesses of the media. Newspapers, radio and television get far fewer letters than most people imagine, and they do have an impact, even if they are not printed. Nobody should give up writing letters to complain where they feel something is justified. Apart from the newspaper Letters pages, each television station, including the BBC, has a permanent 'duty officer' who is on call to record viewers' comments. These are then passed on to the programme makers. Also on television there are more programmes which give the public some sort of access to the airwaves. Channel Four has *Right to Reply*, with their video boxes dotted around the country for viewers to record their own comments. The BBC has *Points of View* and *Open Air*, which as a daily programme gives viewers a real chance to publicise their dissatisfaction.

On local and national radio, there are phone-ins, where complaints and opinions can be made, and the Radio 4 programmes like *Today* and *PM* have regular letters spots for readers' letters.

There are also organisations like the Campaign for Press and Broadcasting Freedom which spend all their time studying the media and exposing its failures. They have been instrumental in maintaining the campaign to get a Right of Reply onto the statute book in

Parliament. In addition, the Labour Party has now formed a Press and Broadcasting Group to continue its review of media policy. As a possible future government, they are looking for ideas for reform.

The next few years are vital for the future of the media. Great technical advances are now established in both the Press and broadcasting. In television and radio it has brought variety and diversity to an industry which before only had a regulated system. The task now is to make sure that the technical advances do not lead to a lowering of standards in an industry which has attracted world acclaim. For the Press, the reverse is true. Even though it has always had the capacity to be diverse, it has been shrinking for the last forty years. Now technical advances have made it possible to reverse that concentration. It needs a bold government to take on the *status quo*, and provide the support necessary to create an industry which makes us proud to say that we really do have a Free Press.

References

Ayerst, D, *The Guardian: A Biography of a Newspaper*. Collins. London. 1971.

Baistow, Tom, *Fourth Rate Estate*, Comedia, 1985.

Benn, Tony, *The Need for a Free Press*, Institute for Workers Control, 1979.

Berry, et al, *Where is the Other News?*, Minority Press Group.

Boyd-Barrett, O, *Journalism Recruitment and Training: Problems in Professionalisation*, Media Sociology, Ed. J. Tunstall, Constable 1970.

Breed, W, Social Control in the Newsroom: A Functional Analysis. Printed in *Structure and Behaviour*, Ed. J. Litterer, VOL I. 1963.

Butler, David, and **Kavanagh**, Dennis, *The British General Election of 1983*. MacMillan.

Campaign for Press and Broadcasting Freedom, *A Labour Daily*, 1984.

Campaign for Press and Broadcasting Freedom, *The Right of Reply*.

Campaign for Press and Broadcasting Freedom, *Media Hits the Pits*, The media and the coal dispute. CPBF, 1984.

Campaign for Press and Broadcasting Freedom, *'Rejoice'*. Media Freedom and the Falklands, CPBF, 1984.

Cleverley, Graham, *The Fleet Street Disaster: British National Newspapers as a Case Study in Mismanagement*, Constable.

Cockerell, Michael, **Hennessy**, Peter, and **Walker**, David, *Sources close to the Prime Minister*, Macmillan London Ltd, 1984.

Cohen, S. and **Young** J. *The Manufacture of News, Deviance, Social Problems and the Mass Media*, London, Constable, 1973.

Crick, Michael, *Scargill and the Miners*, Penguin 1985.

Curran, James, *The British Press: A Manifesto*, Constable 1979.

Curran, James, et al, *Mass Communication and Society*, Arnold 1977.

Curran, and **Seaton**, Jane, *Power without Responsibility*, Fontana.

Driver, Christopher, *The Disarmers*, Hodder and Stoughton, 1964.

Economist Intelligence Unit, *The National Newspaper Industry: A Survey*, London,EIU, 1966.

Evans, Harold, *Good Times, Bad Times*, Wiedenfield and Nicholson, 1983.

Andrew Forrester, *Beyond Our Ken*, Fourth Estate, 1985.

Glasgow University Media Group, *Bad News*, Routledge and Kegan Paul, 1976.

Glasgow University Media Group, *More Bad News*, Routledge and Kegan Paul, 1980.

Glasgow University Media Group, *Really Bad News*, Writers and Readers, 1982.

Golding, Peter, *The Mass Media*, Longman 1974.

Goodhart, David, and **Wintour**, Patrick, *Eddie Shah and the Newspaper Revolution*, Coronet, 1986.

Hamilton, D, *"Who is to own the British Press?"*, Haldane Memorial Lecture, Birbeck College, London, 1976.

Harris, Robert, *The Media, the Government and the Falklands Crisis*, Faber and Faber, 1982.

Hirsch Fred, and **Gordon**, David, *Newspaper Money*, Hutchinson, 1975.

Hollingsworth, Mark, *The Press and Political Dissent*, Pluto, 1986.

Hood, Stuart, *On Television*, Pluto, 1980.

Hood, Stuart, *The Mass Media: Studies in Contemporary Europe.*

Husband, Charles, (Editor). *White Media and Black Britain*, Arrow, 1975.

Koestler, A. *Spanish Testament*, Gollancz, 1937.

Labour Party, *The People and the Media*, 1974.

Leapman, Michael, *The Last Days of the Beeb*, Allen and Unwin, 1986.

MacKay, R, and **Barr**, Brian, *The Story of the Scottish Daily News.* Edinburgh, Canongate, 1976.

MacShane, Denis, *Using the Media*, Pluto, 1982.

Minority Press Group, *The Other Secret Service, Press Distributors and Press Censorship.* Minority Press Group, 1980.

Minority Press Group, *Here is the Other News, Challenges to the Local Commercial Press.* Minority Press Group. 1980.

McQuail, Denis, *Review of Sociological Writing on the Press.* Working Paper No 2 of Royal Commission on the Press. HMSO, 1976.

Pilger, John. *Heroes.* Cape. 1986.

Pimlott, Ben, *Hugh Dalton*, Cape. 1985.

Pimlott, Ben, and **Cook**, C. (Editors). *Trade Unions in British Politics.* Longmans, 1982.

Porter, Henry, *Lies, Damned Lies and Some Exclusives.* Chatto and Windus. 1984.

Press Council. *Press Conduct in the Sutcliffe Case.* Press Council Booklet No 7. 1983.

Robertson, Geoffrey. *People against the Press. An Enquiry into the Press Council.* Quartet Books. 1983.

Royal Commission on the Press. *The Report*, HMSO. 1947.

Royal Commission on the Press. *The Report*, HMSO. 1962.

Royal Commission on the Press. *The Report, Interim Report*. HMSO. 1976.

Royal Commission on the Press. *Industrial Relations in the National Newspaper Industry.* A Report by the Advisory Conciliation and Arbitration Service. HMSO. 1976.

Royal Commission on the Press. *The Report*. 1977.

Seaton Jane, and **Pimlott**, Ben. (Editors). *The Media in British Politics*. Gower Publishing Co. 1987.

Schlesinger, Philip. *Putting 'Reality' Together*. BBC News. Constable. 1978.

Sisson, Keith. *Industrial Relations in Fleet St*. Blackwell. 1975.

Tremayne, Charles. The Social Organisation of Newspaper Houses. *Sociological Review Monograph*. University of Keele. 1980.

Tunstall, Jeremy. *The media in Britain*. Constable 1983.

Tunstall, Jeremy, *Journalists at Work*. Constable. 1977.

Whitaker, Brian. *News Limited. Why you can't read all about it*. Minority Press Group. (no 5). 1981.

Waugh, Evelyn. *Scoop*. Penguin. 1957.